Celebrate!

THE STORY OF THE MUSEUM OF INTERNATIONAL FOLK ART

MUSEUM OF NEW MEXICO PRESS • SANTA FE

The publication of CELEBRATE! was made possible by a grant from the International Folk Art Foundation.

Richard Polese, editor; Rachel Abrams, designer; photography by Art Taylor, Cradoc Bagshaw, E. Johanson, Laura Gilpin, Jim Drum, Sallie Wagner, Chester Maydole, Robert Nugent, and Helga Teiwes.

Post Office Box 2087
Santa Fe, New Mexico 87503

First Edition. *Printed in the United States of America.*

ISBN: 0-89013-119-8
Library of Congress Catalog Card Number 78-78179

On the cover: A Christmas wall hanging, Jul Bonad, *painted by Anders Bengtsson of Smaland, Sweden, 1832. From the International Folk Art Foundation Collection. Photograph by Cradoc Bagshaw.*

Back cover: Miniature violin player made by the Tarahumara people of Batopilas Canyon, Chihuahua, Mexico, 1978. Photograph by Art Taylor.

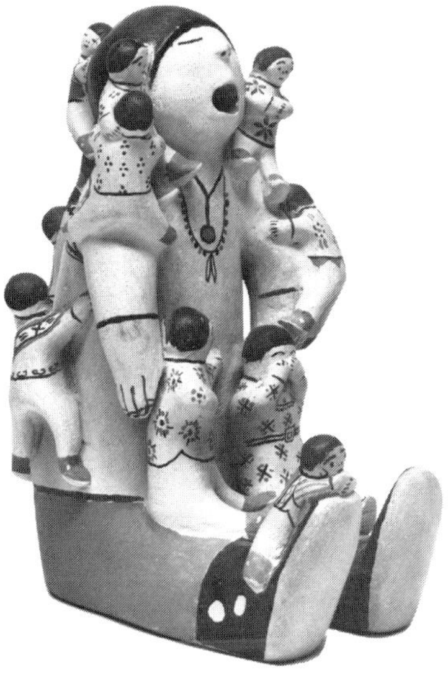

CONTENTS

FOLK ART MUSEUM MARKS TWENTY-FIFTH YEAR

An Introduction

The Museum of International Folk Art is the most recently established of the four main units of the Museum of New Mexico at Santa Fe. With the celebration of its Silver Jubilee, however, we feel it can now lay claim to full maturity.

In this publication there is no attempt to give a detailed account of all the activities that have occurred during the past twenty-five years. The intent, rather, is to convey a sense of the museum's diverse activities and its sustained development; that it occupies an important place in the community; that it serves a constituency that extends well beyond the borders of the State of New Mexico; and that it continues to be dependent on many people and organizations for its successes.

History buffs and others who would like a full account of the museum's beginnings and those members of the community who witnessed them and would care to relive the spirited events that marked its formal opening on September 5, 1953, should consult the issue of EL PALACIO *for that same month.*

It is clear to me that the progress here recorded has not been achieved in isolation. It takes more than a dedicated staff to operate a museum successfully. Growth has come only with joint effort from many directions.

At the public level, the museum has benefited from increased funding and support from the State of New Mexico and from grants awarded by the National

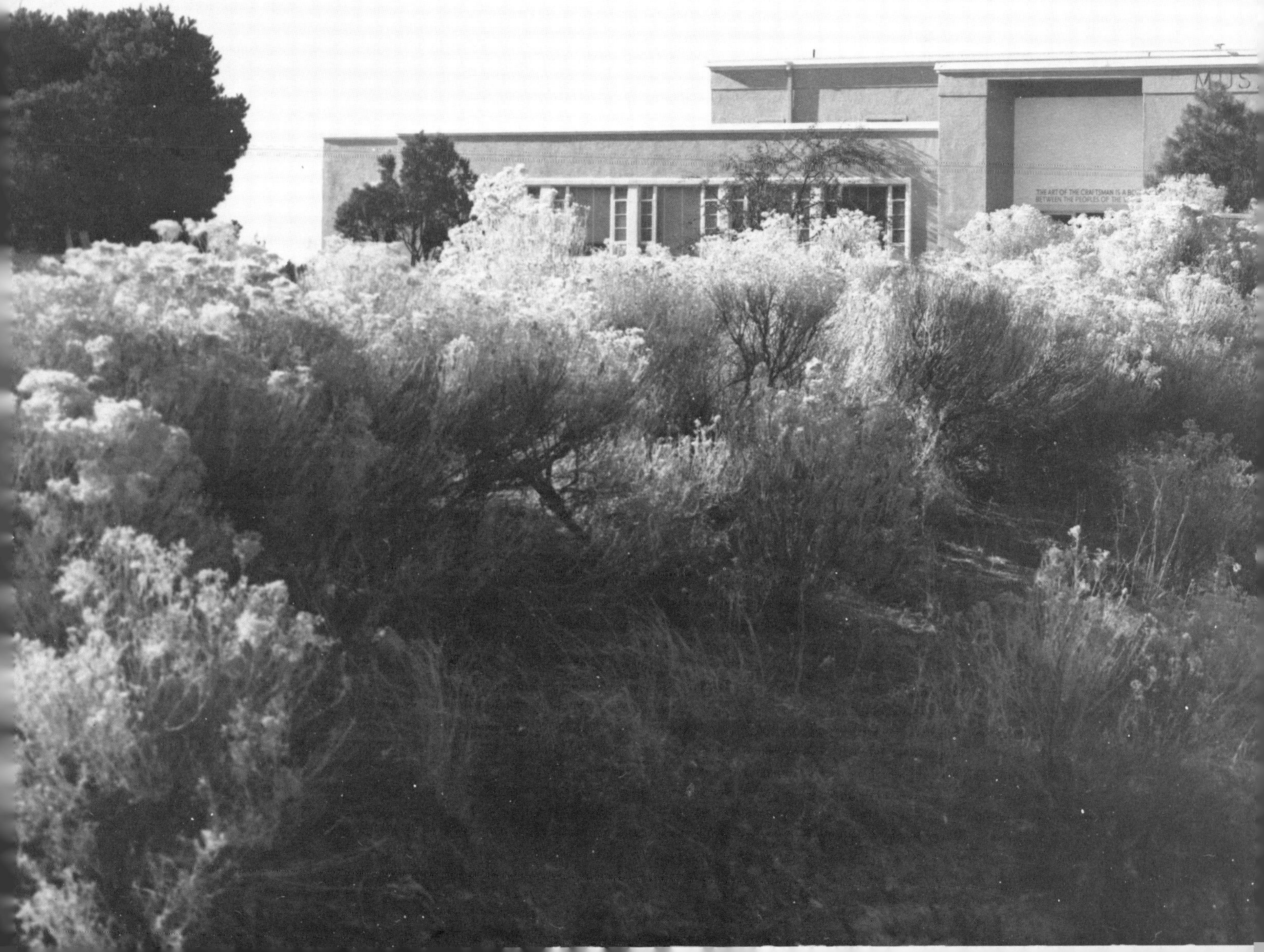

Endowment for the Arts either directly or channeled through the New Mexico Arts Division. At the private level, MOIFA expresses its thanks to those who have served as members of the Board of Regents of the Museum of New Mexico and have guided the museum's development through the years. It recognizes the foresight and prudence of Florence Dibell Bartlett, its founder, in establishing an endowment fund, and acknowledges with gratitude the dedication of those interested and involved persons who have served unselfishly as trustees of the International Folk Art Foundation, charged with administering those funds. The museum is also fortunate in profiting from contributions by the Museum of New Mexico Foundation and from the assistance and support extended by its Folk Art Committee.

Every museum is sustained by volunteer help, and MOIFA is no exception. Countless are the persons who have generously donated their time and labor to perform tasks that have ranged from cleaning leatherworks, polishing silver, stitching fabrics, to conserving specimens, documenting objects, arranging library material, pounding nails and installing exhibits. The Women's Board, a distinguished volunteer organization which maintains the tradition of New Mexican hospitality, deserves a special vote of thanks for arranging friendly receptions at museum functions.

A complete list of all the institutions and individuals who have contributed to the international scope of the collections by gifting objects from many countries would be formidable. Let all of them find here the museum's expression of deep gratitude.

An institution such as the Museum of International Folk Art is similar to a family in many ways. There are comings and goings. Some members record modest successes; others achieve stellar status. They all contribute, however, to the vitality of the organization. It is fitting, therefore, that the hard work, expertise, and dedication of past and present staff be gratefully acknowledged here.

This is an inside view. The reader is invited to judge the museum for himself by visiting our fine building on Camino Lejo in Santa Fe.

Florence Dibell Bartlett was a woman of considerable vision. Let us hope that, furthering her dream, will be the implementation of new development plans which have been triggered in large measure by the extraordinary folk art collection which comes to the museum as a gift from the Girard Foundation of Santa Fe. In the coming years, it will take continued enterprise from many quarters to expand that vision.

Yvonne Lange, Ph.D.
Director
Museum of International Folk Art

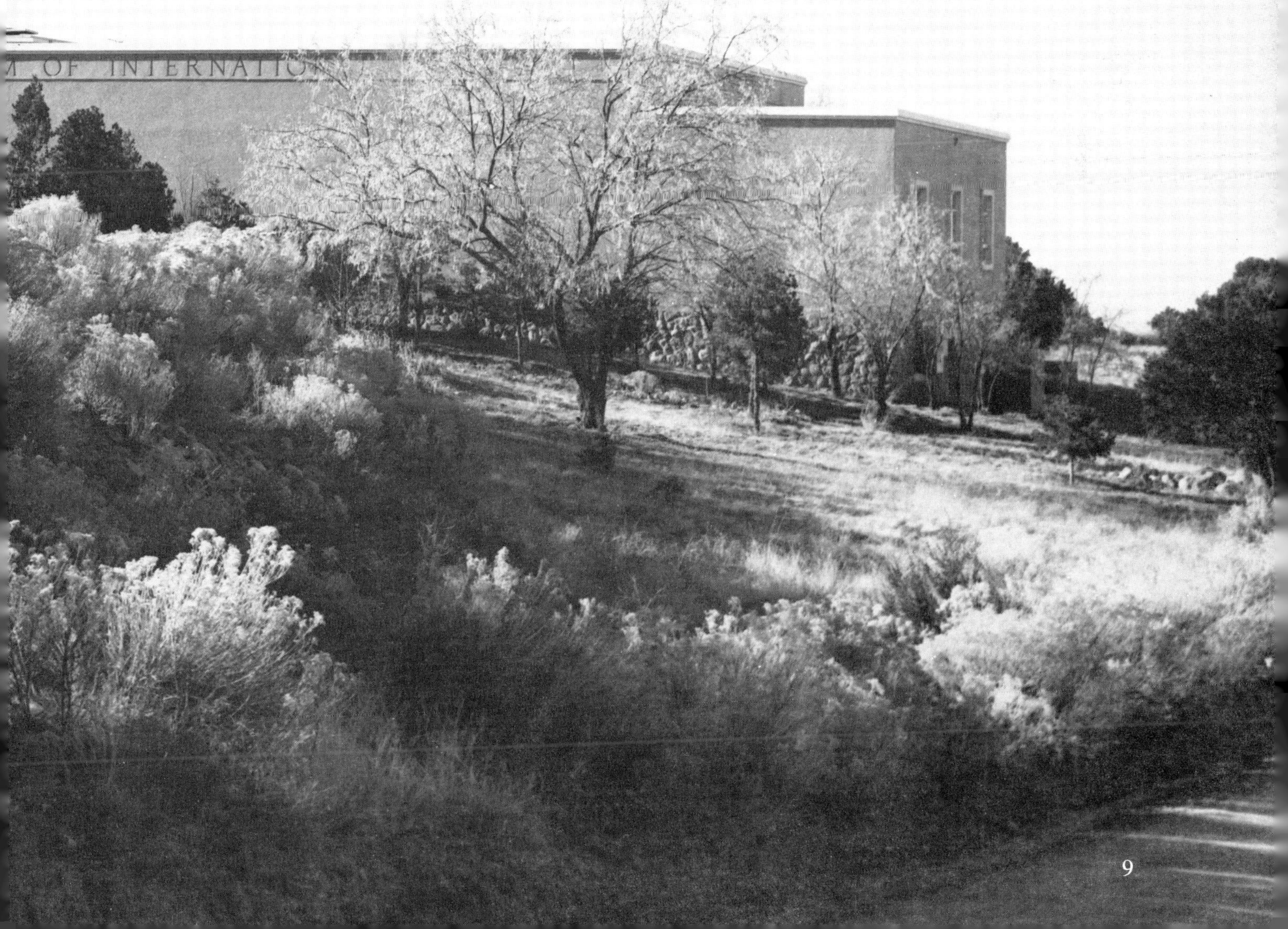

FLORENCE DIBELL BARTLETT:

THE PRIME MOVER in the creation of the Museum of International Folk Art was a very singular lady with a very singular idea.

As MOIFA celebrated its twenty-fifth anniversary this year, it marked also the passing of an equal number of years since the death of its founder, Florence Dibell Bartlett, a woman with an unusually strong and special commitment to promoting social and civic betterment.

Born in Chicago on November 11, 1881, Florence Dibell Bartlett came from a prosperous and well-educated family. Her father, Adolphus Clay Bartlett, had risen—in the best nineteenth century tradition—from a clerical position at age nineteen to secretary and later chairman of the board of the Hibbard, Spencer, Bartlett and Company hardware firm. As befitted a man of his means, he insisted that the three children born to him and his wife, Mary H. Pitkin Bartlett, be sent to the best schools available. Florence was enrolled in Smith College, from which she received a B.L. degree in 1904.

Florence Dibell Bartlett, Director Robert B. Inverarity and French representative Paul Coze unpack gifts from the French government, 1953.

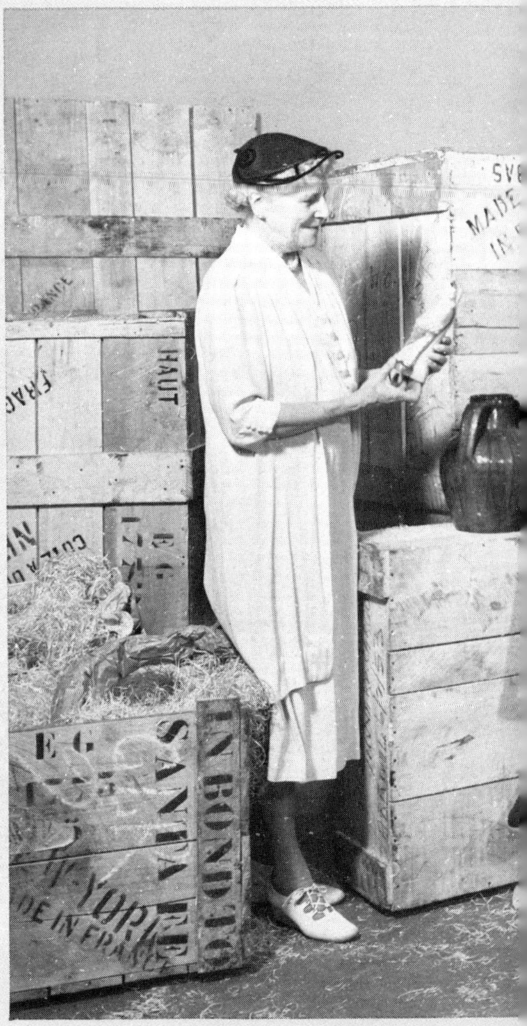

Whether as a result of their education or their father's own example, all three of the Bartlett children exhibited a keen sense of social responsibility as that virtue was perceived in the early twentieth century: to better the lot of the less fortunate through establishment and support of institutions that would make certain opportunities and cultural experiences available to all. Accordingly, Florence embarked on a life as a "civic worker" (preferring that term to "philanthropist") soon after her graduation from college. Her brother, Frederick Clay Bartlett, donated a collection of paintings by the French Impressionists to the Art Institute of Chicago; and her sister and brother-in-law, Maie Bartlett Heard and Dwight B. Heard, established the Heard Museum in Phoenix in 1929.

One of Miss Bartlett's earliest endeavors in improving social conditions was with the Eleanor Association, a Chicago organization that assisted in finding shelter, friends, and worthwhile diversions for young women who came to the city to work. For years she maintained a summer camp for members of this group, organizing entertainment, providing excursions around Lake Michigan, and herself giving inspirational services on Sundays. She also assisted girls who had come before Chicago's Juvenile Court.

Another interest, probably growing out of her love of travel, was the American-Scandinavian Foundation. Her devotion to this organization earned her a gold medal from the King of Sweden in 1933.

A third focus of her attention was the Art Institute of Chicago. Like other members of her family she was an avid art collector, and

THE PRIME MOVER

By Judith Sellars
Librarian,
Museum of International Folk Art

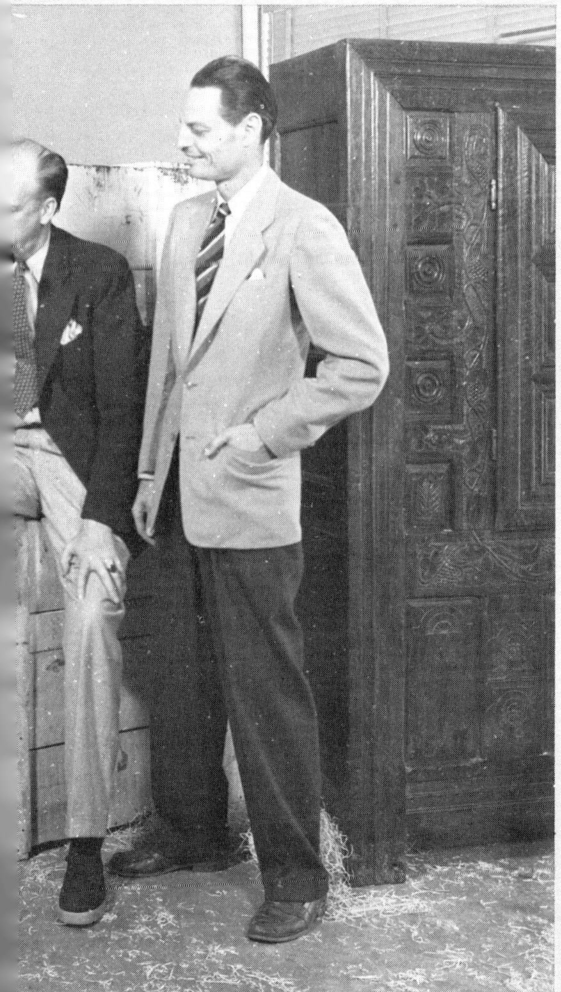

from time to time she lent or donated portions of her collections for exhibition there. For seventeen years she sponsored the weekly Bartlett Lectures, sometimes showing slides herself while dressed in the costume of one country or another. Her generosity established the pension fund at that museum.

Progressively her interests came to lie more with folk art than with the fine arts, although the point in her life at which this change in direction occurred cannot be precisely pinpointed. Throughout her life she was credited with great interest and sympathy toward "common" people; one friend recalled that Florence exhibited real delight when opportunities arose to share everyday labors—even dishwashing! Furthermore, she had begun to travel early, and often enough, so that she had no difficulty in observing various facets of folklife or in obtaining items for her collections. Such interests, she found, were shared by Scandinavian folk museums and a few collectors as well. Her sister in particular was deeply involved in collecting Spanish Colonial and Southwestern Indian art.

Beginning in the 1920s, Florence Bartlett also experienced rural life firsthand, while spending summers at a ranch she acquired in Alcalde, New Mexico.

Village life at Alcalde reinforced what she had observed elsewhere: traditional folk art was diminishing as use of mass-produced goods increased. Her storerooms at the ranch filled as she sought more and more examples of folk art, both from New Mexico and abroad. In *A Tribute to Florence Dibell Bartlett* (International Folk Art Foundation, Santa Fe, 1963), John B. Jackson wrote of her collecting:

> . . . she was neither a trained ethnologist nor an art historian; but, with an instinctive feel for the popular and simple, she collected in the course of years objects of great rarity along with some of everyday availability, handmade objects that were strictly speaking museum pieces, as well as machine made, mass produced articles often little more than imitations or poor adaptations of traditional forms . . . [Her] manner of choosing, far from being haphazard, showed a sure instinct for what was truly living folk art . . .

Preservation in the face of change was, to be sure, an important motive in her collecting, but probably more important were her feelings with respect to what folk art symbolized. Living as she did through two world wars and knowing both the hope stemming from the establishment of the United Nations and the disillusionment engendered by the Cold War, she came to regard folk art as an important aspect of an existing fellowship between national groups. In the early 1950s she elaborated on this theme on Edward R. Murrow's network program, *"This I Believe"*:

> As . . . years passed and extensive journeys were made, I often experienced [a] bond of fellowship between different nationalities . . . , a capacity to appreciate something in one another and to express that vital core of love which lies within the hearts of men and helps to bind them together . . . Perhaps it was my efforts to collect folk art, the art of the common people, which brought me in closer touch with their homes and lives. Gradually this realization grew that if peoples of different countries could have the opportunity to study each others' culture, it would be one avenue for a closer understanding between men.
>
> Today I believe that . . . there can be a closer bond of mutual appreciation between all peoples. It is a conviction founded on the rock of an increased spiritual discernment that an interdependence of nations and a world-encircling unity is possible of realization as each individual upholds this idea and endeavors to demonstrate it in his own life.

By 1948 these convictions had led her to enter into discussions with the Museum of New Mexico regarding her Alcalde ranch and the collections it housed. At first she simply wanted to transform the ranch into a museum much like the Scandinavian outdoor folk museums, but later, when she realized that the cost of such an undertaking would have been too great for the Museum of New Mexico, she agreed to both donate the ranch to the state and finance construction of a new museum building in Santa Fe—the Museum of International Folk Art.

The opening exhibition of pieces from Miss Bartlett's collection was displayed from 1953 through 1956.

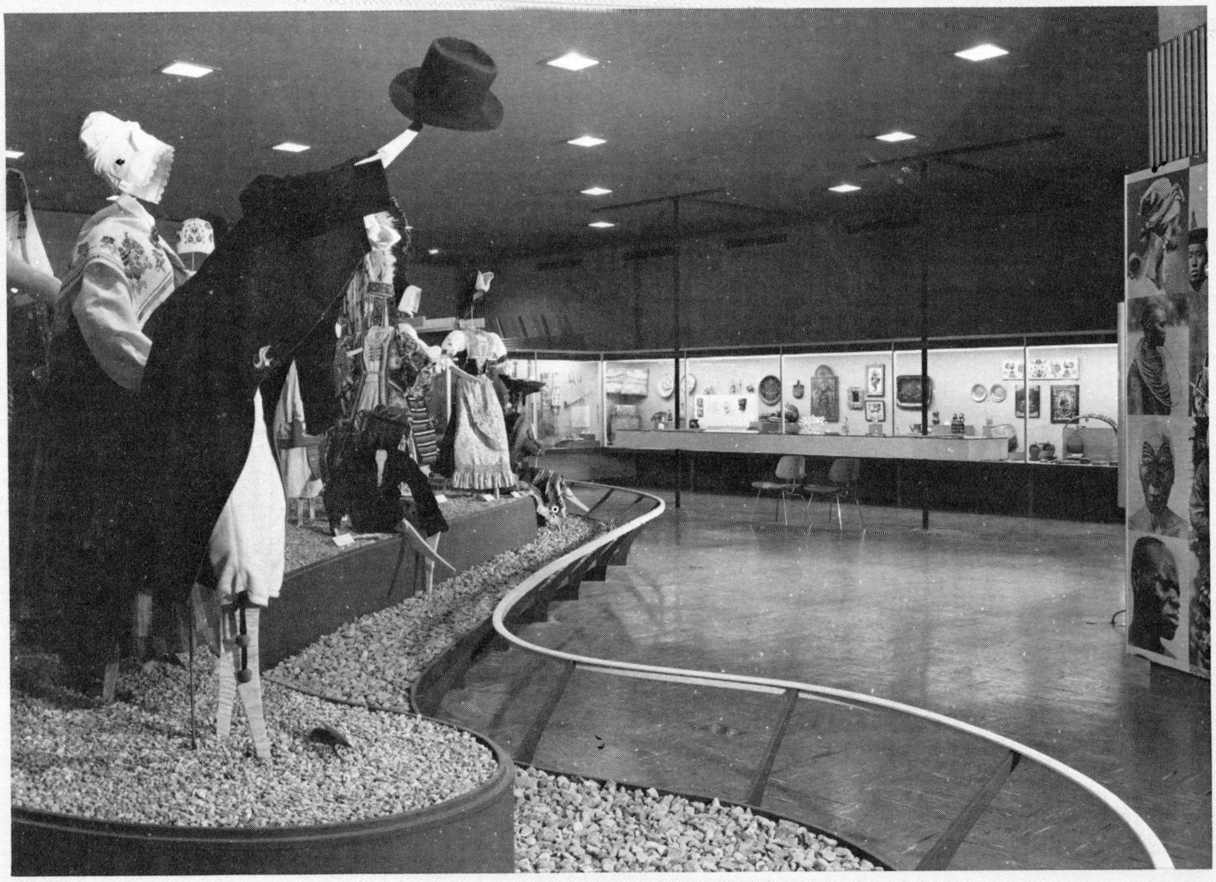

She established and endowed the International Folk Art Foundation as well, in order to assist the museum in carrying out its cultural, educational and public service objectives.

Once the decision to build the museum had been made, Florence Dibell Bartlett devoted tremendous energy to the project. She personally selected the site and approved the design, taking to heart suggestions from staff at other museums and incorporating recommendations for new features such as air conditioning and humidity control. She herself composed the inscription that appears above the museum's entry: *"The art of the craftsman is a bond between the peoples of the world."* And her architect, John Gaw Meem, remembered that she directly followed up on every one of fifty-three items of correction that arose in the two years between the building's completion and its formal opening. She, of course, was present for that event, held September 5, 1953, and was a central figure in the surrounding national and international interest and acclaim.

Successful as her plans eventually proved, the strain of five years of effort toward the museum's establishment may have exacted a heavy price. When Florence arrived in Santa Fe for Christmas, 1953, friends noted that she seemed preoccupied and failing, a marked change from her usual attentive, cheerful and vigorous self. A few months later, on May 2, 1954, her sudden death shocked everyone.

Florence Dibell Bartlett's passing prompted many tributes, not only from those who had benefitted from her generosity but also from those who believed in her vision and admired her purpose. None, however, matched the precision and succinctness of Edward R. Murrow's assertion: "[She] put her love of folk art and her fellow humans into practice."

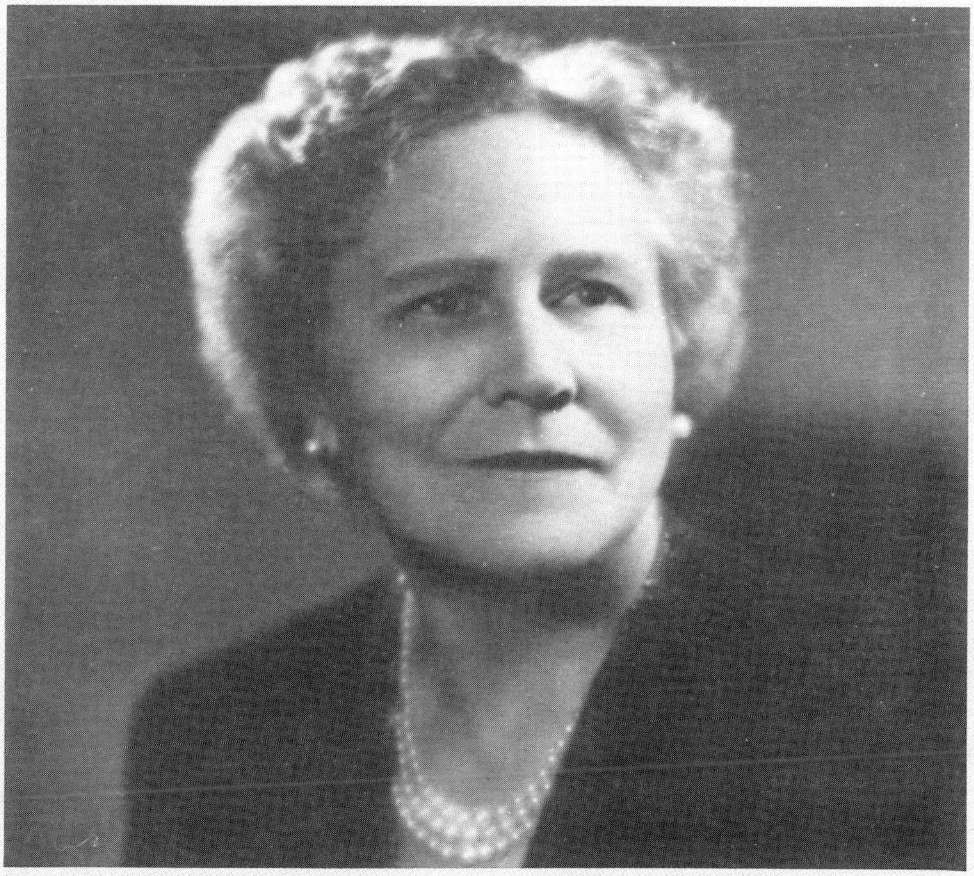

Florence Dibell Bartlett, founder of the Museum of International Folk Art.

Look inside the operation at MOIFA and

HIGHLIGHTS OF A LIVELY

THE MUSEUM OF INTERNATIONAL FOLK ART owes its beginnings to a few colcha embroideries. In the fall of 1948, Boaz Long, Director of the Museum of New Mexico, was in Chicago on business and decided to call on Florence Dibell Bartlett at her home to see if she might be persuaded to make a gift of the New Mexican colchas she had recently lent the Museum. Miss Bartlett's response was to hedge a bit—though graciously—and promise a decision in the near future.

Boaz Long returned to his office in Santa Fe unaware of the ideas his visit had inspired. He, like everyone else, knew that Florence Bartlett was a wealthy and generous art collector with close ties to the museum world and strong feelings about folk art, but this knowledge hardly prepared him for the surprise contained in her reply. Miss Bartlett was indeed willing to donate her colchas—as well as her ranch at Alcalde and her international collections—provided that the Museum would convert the ranch into the type of outdoor folk museum she had often visited in Scandinavia and that the Museum of New Mexico would fund the museum's operation.

Boaz Long had an answer for Miss Bartlett within weeks: the conversion would cost $400,000, and annual operation would run no less than $25,000. The Museum could not afford such large expenditures, and besides, Alcalde was an isolated and out-of-the-way place for a museum.

Miss Bartlett was only partly daunted by this news. For some weeks she apparently mulled over one alternative—converting and operating the ranch as a museum at her own expense. She also consulted René d'Harnoncourt, director of the Museum of Modern Art in New York, about another possibility: locating her museum in Santa Fe. He offered enough encouragement with regard to this prospect that she cabled Boaz Long in early March, 1949:

> . . . I am willing to place museum on your property in the vicinity of Laboratory if large enough eventually to have center there and small foreign houses. I will give ranch to you to sell using your proceeds for endowment of museum.

THE STATE ACCEPTS THE GIFT

Long wasted no time in acting on this offer. He pressed Judge Oliver Seth into drafting a bill for the Legislature, already in session, to accept this gift. The Legislature reacted with similar speed: they charged the Museum of New Mexico with conducting further negotiations with Miss Bartlett and authorized an appropriation to maintain the ranch and promote the objectives of an International Folk Art Museum.

These actions had a very positive effect with Miss Bartlett. In early April 1949 she wrote the Museum that she would consider sites near the Laboratory of Anthropology for her museum, stipulating that she wanted the noted John Gaw Meem of New Mexico as architect for the project. Further, she would bear the expenses for the museum's construction herself and set aside $100,000 for its maintenance.

By late April, Miss Bartlett had selected the site on land donated to the Museum of New Mexico by the late Amelia White. By August, Meem was well into the preliminary plans. It developed, however, that Scandinavian outdoor folk museums would not do as proper models after all. Not only would the cost have been prohibitive, but also the various examples of folk architecture Miss Bartlett proposed to move to the site would have been out of their element, particularly since they could not easily have been screened from one another with suitable vegetation in arid Santa Fe.

Since Miss Bartlett was paying for the museum, she could have largely what she wished, although her plans were subject to approval by the Museum of New Mexico Board of Regents. And what she wanted, it became apparent, was a building that would further her beliefs about the importance of folk art as a vehicle for world understanding and, equally important, provide for a functional museum. That she was interested in more than just a monument to herself became quite

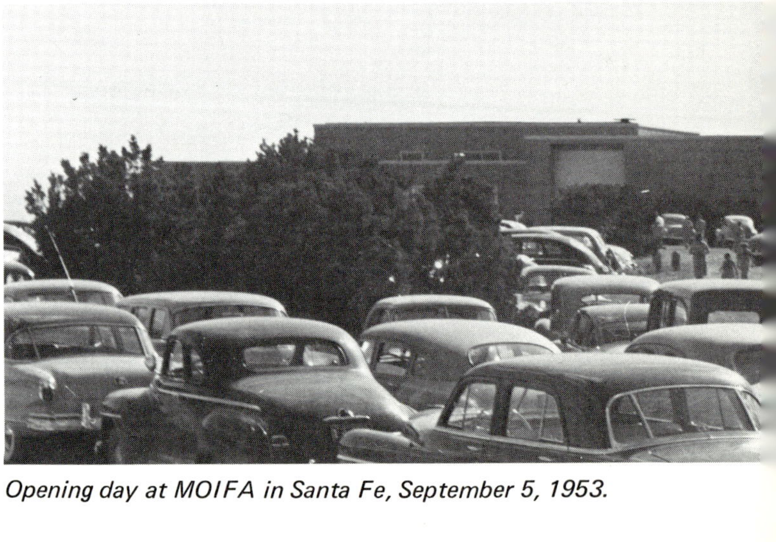

Opening day at MOIFA in Santa Fe, September 5, 1953.

discover an energetic and devoted museum.

FIRST TWENTY-FIVE YEARS

By Judith Sellars and Janet Langlois

clear when she was asked for a portrait to be used in an El Palacio article about people important to the Museum of New Mexico. She declined to send one, advising the editor to run a picture of the museum she was building and a description of its purpose instead, for, in her view, they were of greater consequence than the founder.

A DIRECTOR IS SELECTED

Miss Bartlett's method of deciding what features would be included in the building showed a remarkable capacity for planning and even today would be an adequate model for the museum design process. She knew what she could afford, and she had in mind specific goals the museum was to serve, without being inflexible about how they could be achieved. She respected the opinions of both her architect and Boaz Long and managed to maintain harmonious relationships with them throughout the project. Early on she appointed an advisory board composed of well-known museum directors and individuals with strong connections to museums. With this group's guidance she found qualified persons to review the preliminary sketches, even selecting one of the strongest critics, Dr. Robert Bruce Inverarity, to be the new museum's director. Soon after he had been confirmed in this position, she sent him off on a tour of American and Canadian museums, plans in hand. He conferred with no less than sixteen main advisers on this trip, including architects, museum directors, and curators in the largest and most important museums visited. He returned with a long list of suggestions which were then incorporated in the two revisions of the plans that occurred prior to preparation of the working drawings and specifications.

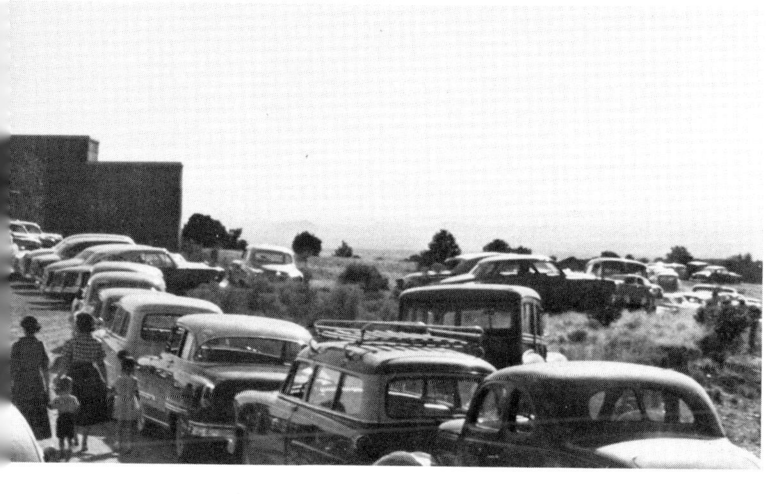

Construction began on August 14, 1950. More than a year was required to complete the basic structure sufficiently that collections and the newly-hired staff could be moved in. While work proceeded on the interior, the staff set about accessioning Miss Bartlett's collection as well as other gifts—nearly 4,000 items in all. They photographed, fumigated, and cleaned or conserved each object. They also planned and built the Museum's initial exhibitions. All these tasks took nearly two years to complete; during that time the Museum remained closed to the public, except for one day in July 1952 when an open house was held for the people of Santa Fe.

On Saturday, September 5, 1953, a well-publicized dedication and opening was held. Some 1,200 eager visitors, including official representatives of foreign countries, state and federal dignitaries, and representatives of universities and other museums, were present. Hundreds squeezed into the auditorium to hear Miss Bartlett present the museum to the State and to watch her cut a ribbon to the galleries. Governor Edwin Mechem of New Mexico added his remarks and was followed by representatives of the governments of France and Finland, who discussed the new museum's significance in the light of better world understanding. Visitors who were not inclined to hear speeches wandered about the museum's first exhibitions—lively arrangements of objects from Miss Bartlett's own collections. They found refreshments plentiful and the presence of a group of Mexican folk musicians invigorating. Activities continued at the Fine Arts Museum that evening when three of the nation's leading anthropologists participated in a forum on primitive art, folk art, and fine art. For pure excitement and impact, probably no Santa Fe opening since has matched that day.

THE BUILDING IN SANTA FE

The site chosen by Miss Bartlett for the Museum of International Folk Art can only be described as a spectacular one. A juniper and piñon-covered rise southeast of Santa Fe's plaza, it affords vast panoramas of plains and mesas and of the Sangre de Cristo, Jemez, Sandia, and Ortiz mountains. In winter, snow weights its piñons—so eagerly shaken by nut harvesters in the fall—and in the summer, rabbits and lizards race through its chamisa while jays scold each intruder to the nearby tranquil arroyos.

The building by John Gaw Meem was designed to harmonize with, rather than dominate, its setting. Built mostly at ground level, it echoes a local Greek Revival variation known as Territorial style with its simple cornice and colored stucco—in dusty pink trimmed with white and yellow. Native stone faces both the foundations and retaining walls.

The interior of the building was inspired by the 1950s "International" style, and today after twenty-five years and numerous repaintings and some remodeling, it still possesses most of the detail that makes it identifiable as a building erected in the early 1950s. Its clean lines and blond woods, unobtrusive lighting, and brushed aluminum door and window frames were originally complemented by blond Scandinavian "modern" furniture and bright draperies; surprisingly, many of the original furnishings remain in good shape and continue in use alongside less harmonious metal office furniture.

When completed in 1953, the structure offered 7,892 square feet of exhibition area and 10,926 square feet of storage. This was augmented in 1970 by an addition of 11,138 square feet, equally divided between basement storage and ground-level exhibition areas. Renovations undertaken during 1976-77 were directed toward improvement, but not expansion, of exhibition space. After the entire building was re-roofed, the configuration of galleries was changed by piercing three new doorways in one wall and the creation of a central hall. Large galleries were also refitted so that they may be divided into smaller galleries as occasion demands.

Even though the building remains a pleasing one, and even though the needs of exhibitions and storage have been met over the past twenty-five years, it cannot be denied that the building has become inadequate in some respects. Basement storage areas do not conform to recently revised fire codes and are now crowded and unhandy as well—situations incompatible with the goal of preservation of the museum's objects. Staff members, their numbers having grown in response to a five-fold increase in collections, lack real offices and consequently have their desks in chilly storage areas where they have been known to wear long underwear and mittens in winter. Visiting researchers have no place to work. The library must double as a meeting room. The conservation laboratory is too small. These problems—only a few among many—were addressed in great detail by architect-planner Verner Johnson in 1977, and plans have subsequently been drawn by architect Harvey Hoshour for an addition to house the Girard Foundation Collection and also remodeling and expansion of the original structure. With these changes, the building should prove as adequate over the next twenty-five years as the present structure fortunately has been during the museum's first quarter century.

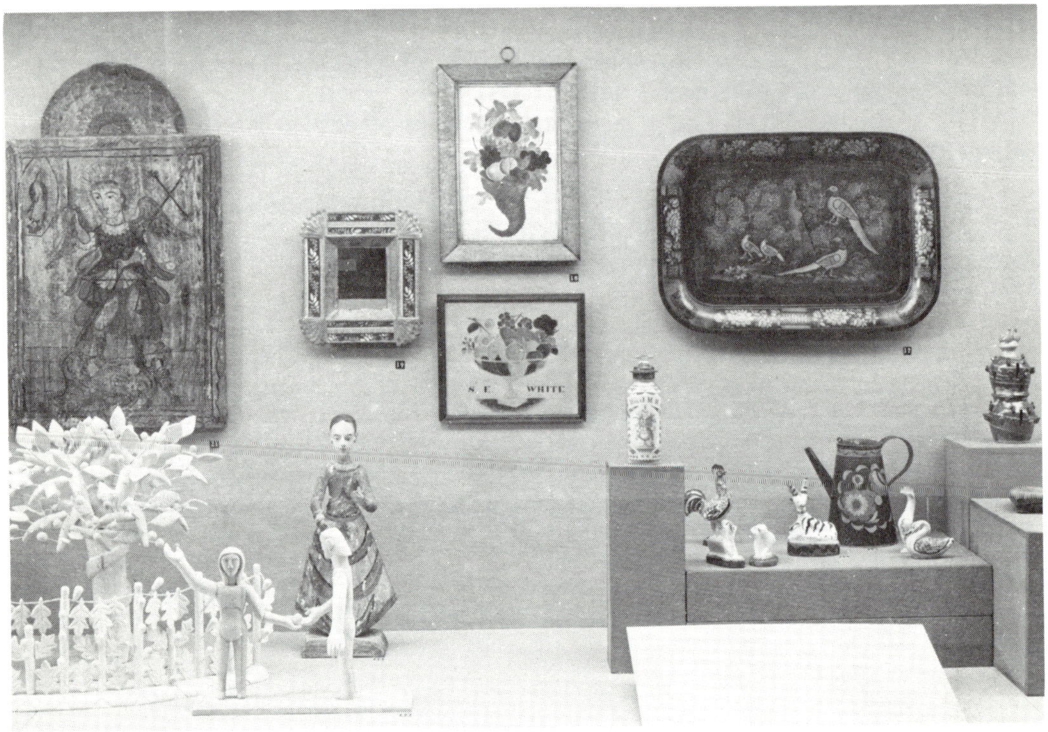

From the beginning the MOIFA staff has stressed the quality of its exhibitions, as in this display from the opening Bartlett Collection show.

A FOUNDATION FOR FOLK ART

When the museum officially opened its doors in September 1953, the International Folk Art Foundation had already been in existence for two years. This non-profit, tax-free corporation was established by Florence Dibell Bartlett, who also served as president of its eight-member board of trustees. It has been perpetuated by her generosity through a trust. Its articles of incorporation detail the Foundation's purpose:

> This corporation is formed for scientific and educational purposes specifically to broaden the study of folk art as related to all countries and so

augment a better understanding among the peoples of the world. Its objects are:

1. To assist financially the Museum of International Folk Art in Santa Fe, New Mexico and in furthering its educational program.
2. To provide funds for increasing the folk art material for exhibitory and study purposes.
3. To assist in building up an adequate museum library.
4. To consider and maintain a proposed museum of peasant cottages and related activities in connection with the museum. (This item was later discarded.)
5. To make contacts with the governments, peoples and museums of other countries that will help to increase the international aspect of the Museum of International Folk Art in Santa Fe.
6. To consider ways and means for publications by the Museum of International Folk Art.

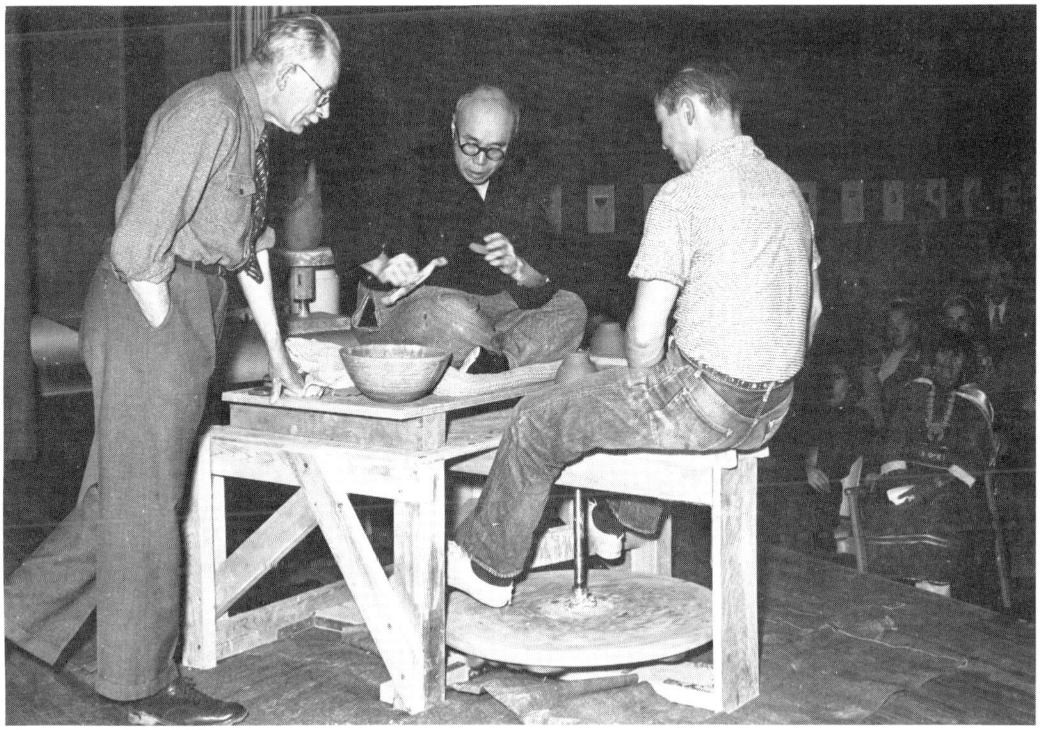

"Craftsmanship Today" demonstration series (1952) featured potters Bernard Leach, Shoiji Hamada and Warren Gilbertson. Maria Martinez observes from the front row.

7. To make a financial plan for traveling exhibitions.
8. To encourage gifts for any of the above named projects and for the foregoing purposes and the objectives of the Museum of International Folk Art.

The Foundation's commitment and support over the years have given the museum both stability and incentive and have allowed its collections to grow significantly in quality as well as quantity. Each year the Foundation normally approves grants to the museum in several of the following areas:

Programs. The museum traditionally schedules a number of lectures, musical events and film showings each year. Especially familiar to the people of Santa Fe over the past several years have been the Sunday afternoon series of films, all of which have related to folk art and folklife. Rented films or those selected from the museum's own collection of one hundred films are shown, with admission charge being kept at a minimum. These activities, however, are being curtailed over the next few years, with the auditorium temporarily in use as a processing center for the Girard Foundation Collection material.

Exhibitions. With folk art exhibitions being far more costly than any others mounted by the Museum of New Mexico, both in terms of materials and man-hours required, the Foundation has often covered all or part of the installation costs of various museum exhibitions.

Demonstrations and workshops. Miss Bartlett held a strong belief that the museum should be more than an exhibition center—that it should further the *practice* of folk crafts as well. In MOIFA's early years, demonstrations of various crafts were invariably held at the museum itself, but more recently the Foundation has also provided funds for instructors to go out to rural areas to teach skills.

Library. Resources for identification and documentation of objects that comprise the collections being essential to a museum, the Foundation grants sufficient funds to the MOIFA library to cover its entire operation. Solely because of the Foundation's interest the library is able to maintain a high level of acquistions.

Publications. In twenty-five years the Foundation has sponsored publication of some fifty catalogs, books and booklets. Many of these publications have resulted from research done under grants from the Foundation.

Research projects. Several scholars and staff members have furthered knowledge of various aspects of folk art as recipients of grants from the Foundation.

Personnel. The State of New Mexico's appropriations for staff salaries, though increasing, have not been adequate to meet the need for personnel to deal with routine handling and processing of MOIFA's collections, administrative program development, library operations, and collections research. Over the past several years the Foundation has funded as many as four positions to ensure the museum's efficient operation. It also provides funds for the staff to attend annual meetings of their professional organizations.

Acquisitions. Staff recommendations for purchases and acceptance of gifts are referred to a Foundation committee which handles funds for acquisitions. During some years, minor purchases have filled in several areas of the collections; in other years, a major acquisition—such as that of the Cordry Collection of Mexican Indian costumes—has meant that little else could be purchased.

The Foundation, then, has helped finance nearly every phase of MOIFA's routine activity, yet its support has not ended there by any means. From 1957 to 1970 it provided funds for traveling exhibitions units, small displays of the museum's collections which were viewed by more than a million New Mexico citizens and visitors. Ownership of these units was transferred to the Museum of New Mexico in 1970, and the project continues to operate today. In 1969-70 a wing for exhibitions and storage was added to the museum at the Foundation's expense. Active encouragement for MOIFA's acquisition of the Girard Foundation Collection began a few years later, after the Foundation had financed an extensive feasibility study. In 1976 it contributed heavily toward the renovation of the main exhibit gallery. And with more renovations and construction on the horizon in the twenty-fifth anniversary year, it has pledged even more assistance and has lent its support in the museum's search for federal and private funds.

CREATING THE EXHIBITIONS

Attendance at the museum has grown steadily, ranging between 65,000 and 82,000 visitors annually during the past eight years. All but a fraction of these visitors see only the exhibitions, and few of them probably ever imagine the planning and work involved in putting an exhibition together.

Years in advance, the staff decides on the themes of forthcoming exhibitions and works out a time schedule with the Exhibitions Bureau, which builds displays for all the museum units administered by the Museum of New Mexico. The staff members responsible for the exhibition then begin necessary research, sometimes undertaking an extensive borrowing of objects and sometimes spending as much as two or three years in full-time study. Once their research objectives have been met, they select from the objects studied those to be displayed. They review their selection with the people at the Exhibitions Bureau, so that the latter can then set about working on the exhibition's design. Museum staff members next write the labels and other text for the exhibition; if a catalog is involved, they may already have been busy preparing it for some time. Meanwhile, the exhibitions staff builds cases, stands and other structures, paints, prepares the labels, and installs the objects in the various displays. Work often proceeds almost to the very hour that the exhibition opens, and the calmness that the museum and

"Navajo Pictorial Weaving: An American Folk Art" (1975-76) displayed these fascinating pictorial rugs and many others.

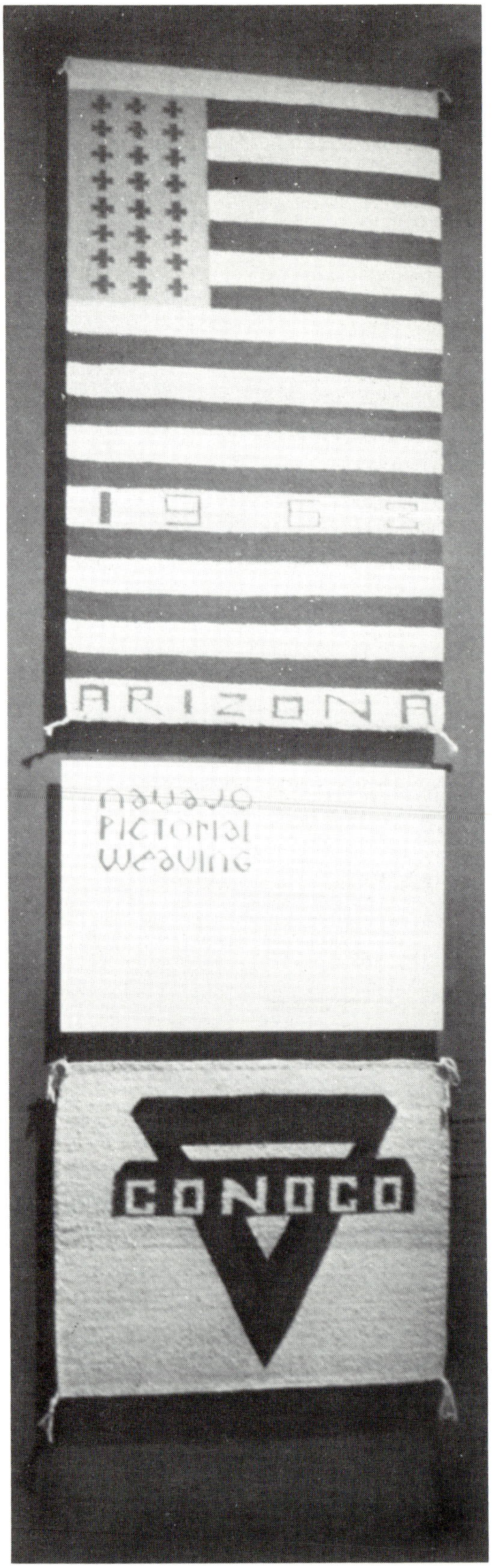

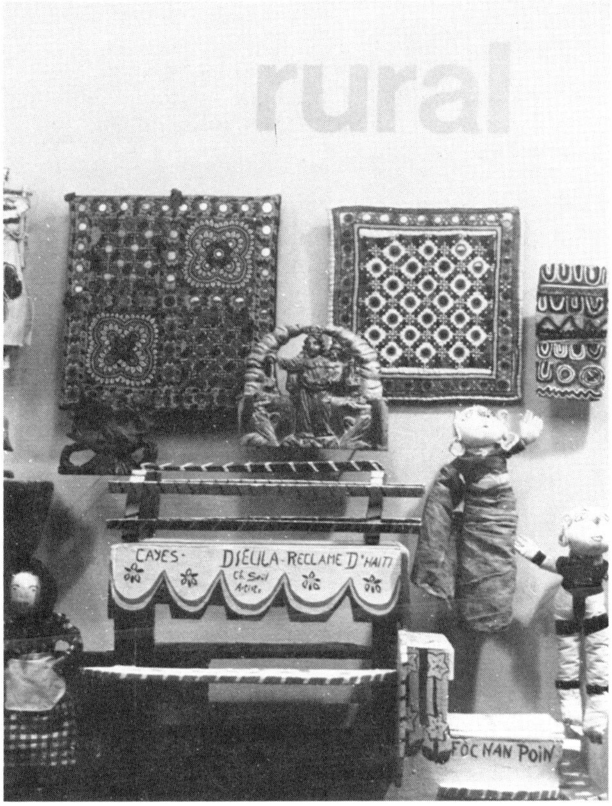

Above: Pieces from "What Is Folk Art?" (1973-76).

Below: Victorian set in the exhibition, "Fantasy and Enchantment: Selections from the Girard Foundation Collection."

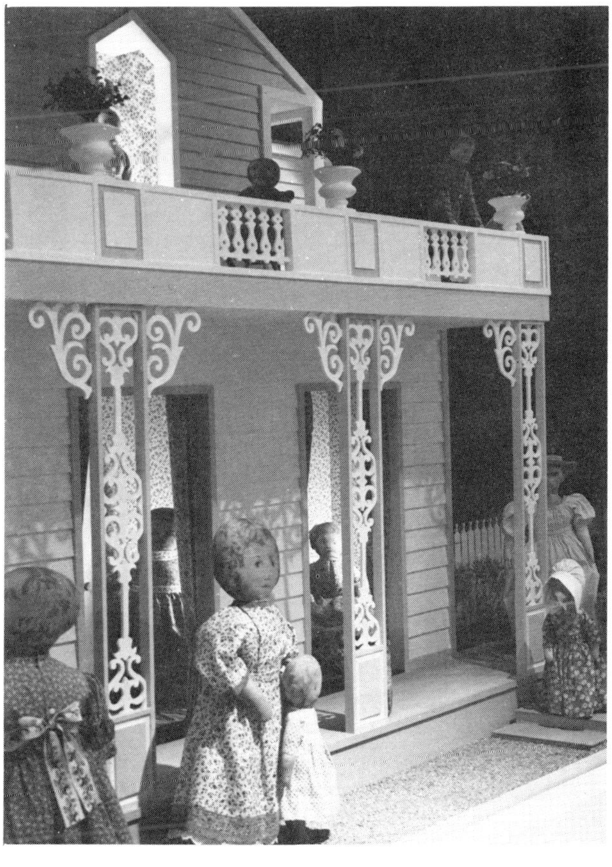

exhibitions staffs seem to show at openings is frequently not calmness at all, but extreme fatigue!

This process has been repeated at least four or five times per year over the past twenty-five years. Whether an exhibition has been a major one or a smaller one, however, each presentation has contributed to the variety of the 167 exhibitions held at the museum over the 1953-1978 period. From all these a few basic types of exhibitions have been discerned:

A single folk art in many places. Several exhibitions have dealt with similarities and differences in one type of object from various cultures. One of the most memorable was "Nacimientos," loaned, designed and installed by Alexander Girard in 1961. To this day, many of those who viewed this sensitive display of Christmas Cribs and were moved by its Biblical message inquire about the possibility of a repeat exhibition.

"The Shape of Music," 1965-66, used folk musical instruments from West Africa, Turkey, Iran, Italy, Egypt and Greece to illustrate that instruments unique in shape and material nevertheless employ common principles in their production of music: wind, percussion, resonance and strings.

"Folk Art in Wood," 1968-69, developed the concept of the universality of wood—adaptable and available almost everywhere—as a folk art medium. Beginning with a panel of eighty kinds of timber keyed to a world map, the exhibition displayed both an array of tools used in making wooden objects and the objects themselves: vehicles, such as a Sicilian painted cart and a New Mexican *carreta,* and weapons, including an Irish club, a Spanish lance, and a nineteenth-century Pennsylvania rifle. A "universal kitchen," filled with wooden bowls, spoons, butter churns, grinding boards, and cookie molds, plus a cross-section of an adobe Spanish Colonial home, with its wooden *vigas* (log beams), corbels and wooden furniture, offered further examples of the contexts in which wooden implements are used throughout the world.

"World of Folk Costume," 1971-73, examined the structure, ornamentation, and function of costume. Garments ranging from a silk sarong to an ornate Czechoslovakian festival dress illustrated a progression from simple rectangular and cylindrical forms to elaborately cut and patterned clothing. Other costumes were arranged to show surface ornamentation: coloring techniques, such as tie-dye, painting, batik, ikat, and stencil; embroidery, including goosequill, metal, and fibers; and other techniques, such as applique, beading, patchwork, and machine stitch. Still other costumes were examples of the social functions of dress in identifying the wearer's occupation or status: a wedding dress, an Indian ghost dance dress, a pilgrim's jacket, and a Chinese actor's robe. The community identity of the individual was illustrated by costumes designed to show dress variation within a particular region. Clothing from three parishes in Dalarna Province, Sweden; from six villages in the state of Oaxaca, Mexico; and from Palestinian villages near Jerusalem, served for comparison.

A single folk art in a single place. Many exhibitions have been of a specific folk art within a particular region. Standing out in this category is "Chinese

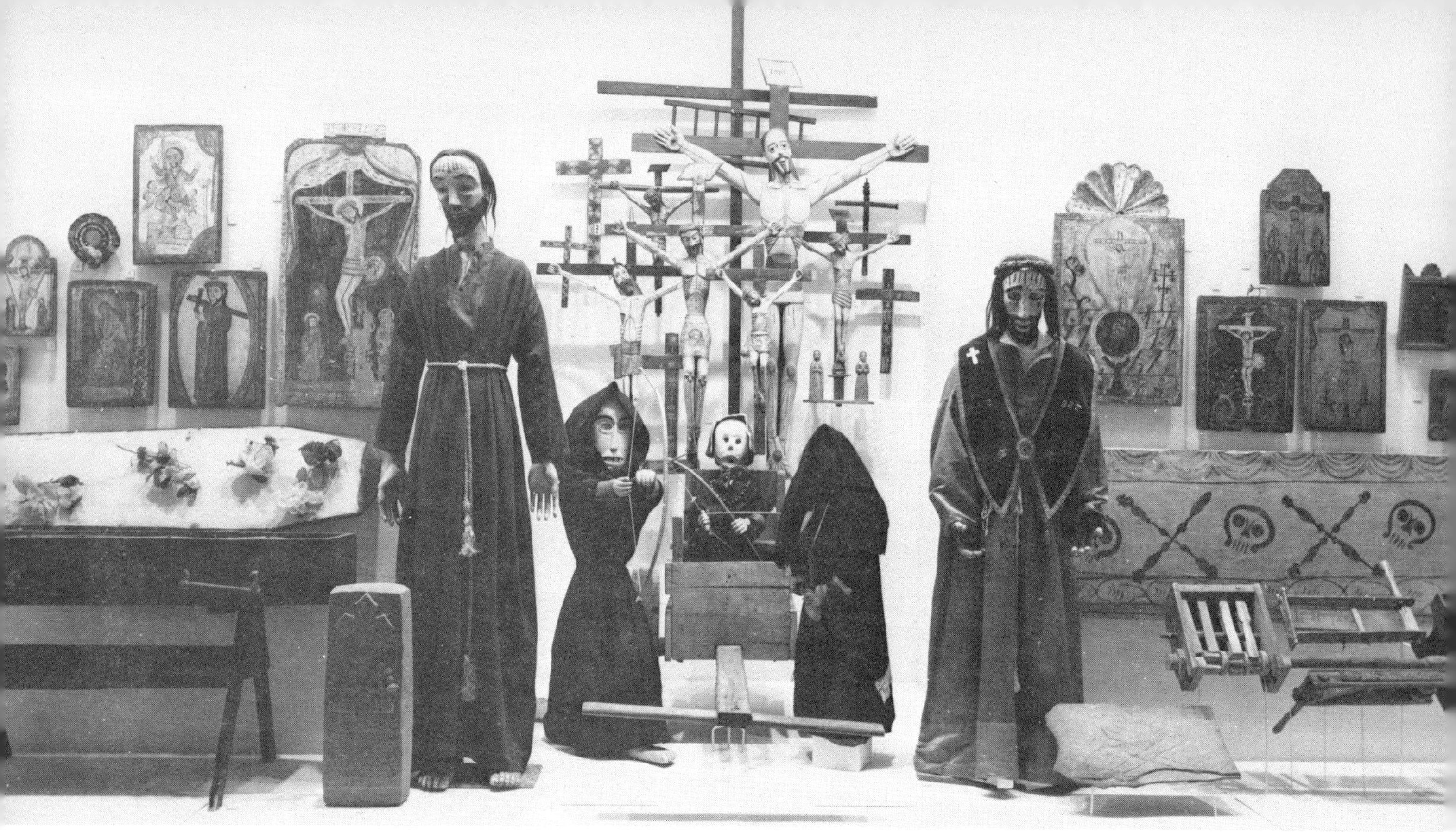

"Días de Más, Días de Menos: Spanish Folklife and Art in New Mexico" included splendid religious carvings and paintings from the mountain villages.

Peasant Cottons," 1964, which concentrated on the ancient western Chinese art of decorating coarse cotton fabrics with embroidered, stenciled and dyed motifs. Antique pieces as well as modern adaptations, including bed valances, bedspreads, trousseau pillow cases, clothing, and samplers, were shown.

Another exhibition, "Navajo Pictorial Weaving," 1975-76, examined pictorial design motifs in Navajo weaving, once discouraged because they fetched lower prices than geometric patterns. A few stubborn Navajo women, however, paid little attention to the market and continued to transfer their fascination with American society—especially its technology—into their textiles. The 107 weavings used in this exhibition depicted trains, trucks, automobiles, advertising logos, cartoon characters, and Christmas trees.

General folk art of a single place. Several exhibitions have presented examples of the folk crafts practiced in a particular country or specific region. The Abby Aldrich Rockefeller Collection show, "American Folk Art," 1963, was an outstanding example. Portraits in oil, weather vanes, figureheads, tradesmen's symbols, toys and gimcracks combined to convey a sense of nostalgia for the "good old days" of this country's past.

"Swedish Folk Art," 1964, is another example. Over 500 handcrafted items, including fine linens, "*Bonader*" (wall paintings of Biblical scenes), and Lapp art, showed the continuity of tradition in Sweden from the peak craft period, 1750-1850, to the twentieth-century revival movement. This collection, circulated in the United States by the Smithsonian Institution, was sponsored jointly by the Nordiska Museet in Stockholm, the Swedish Institute for Cultural Relations, and the Swedish Embassy. It was complemented by the Museum of International Folk Art's own holdings in Scandinavian artifacts.

General folk art of a single place related to folk art of many places. The unique "Afro-Arabic" exhibition, 1966-67, showed the relationship of Spanish Colonial art to its international prototypes. The show was designed to illustrate the influence of Islamic culture on New Mexico by way of the cultures of Asia Minor, the Arabian Peninsula, North and West Africa, and finally Spain. The cosmopolitan atmosphere of an African bazaar was an effective medium for displaying examples of the diverse cultural types that have contributed distinct elements to the creation of Spanish Colonial art in New Mexico.

General folk art of many places related to definition of a concept. Over 900 items were displayed in another one-of-a-kind exhibition, "What is Folk Art?" (1973-76). Here the aim was to invite the museum goer to ponder over stereotyped notions about the nature of folk art, to show that questions may generate conflicting responses, and to emphasize that a neat, compact

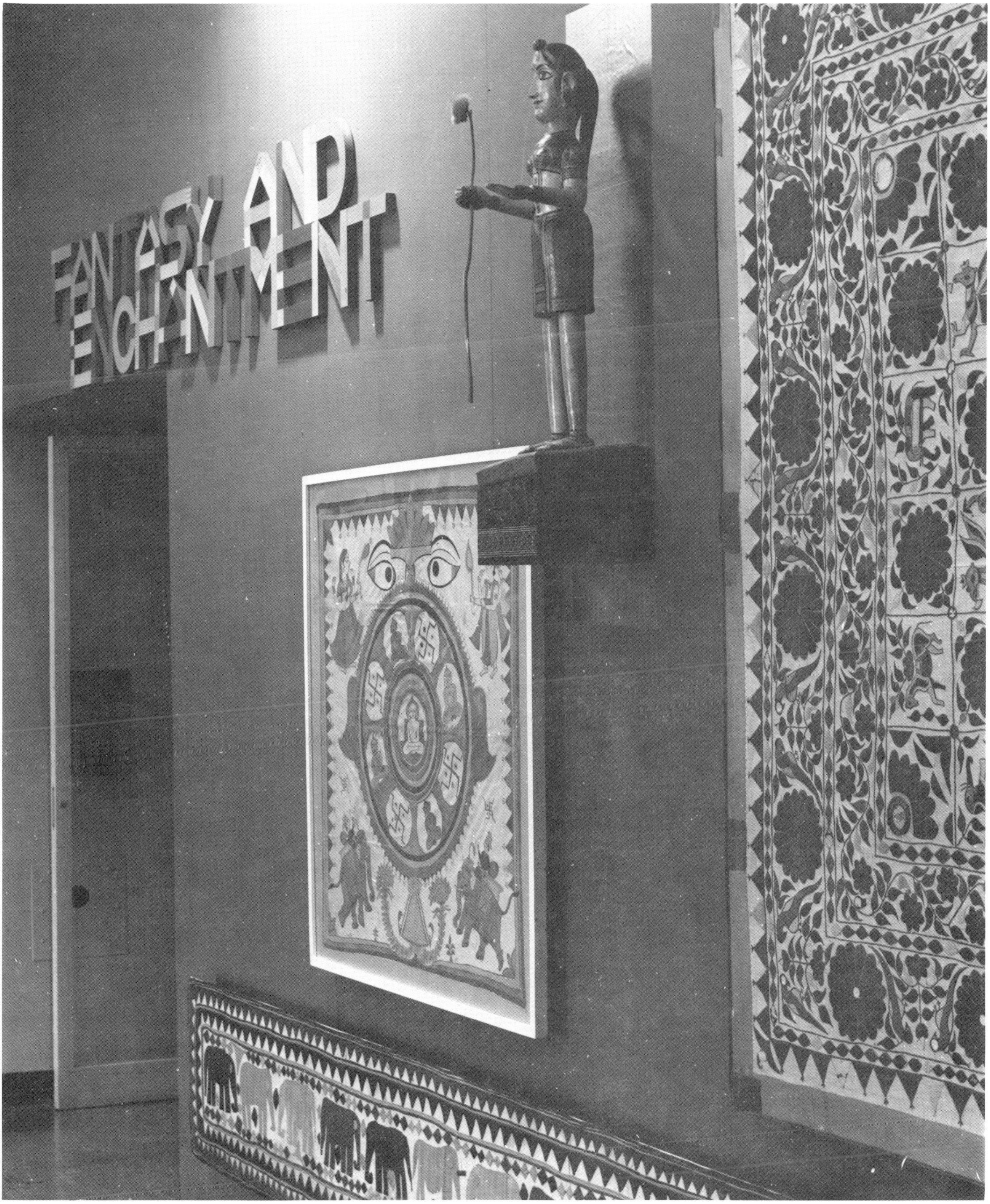

Entrance to "Fantasy and Enchantment: Selections from the Girard Foundation Collection" which opened in 1977.

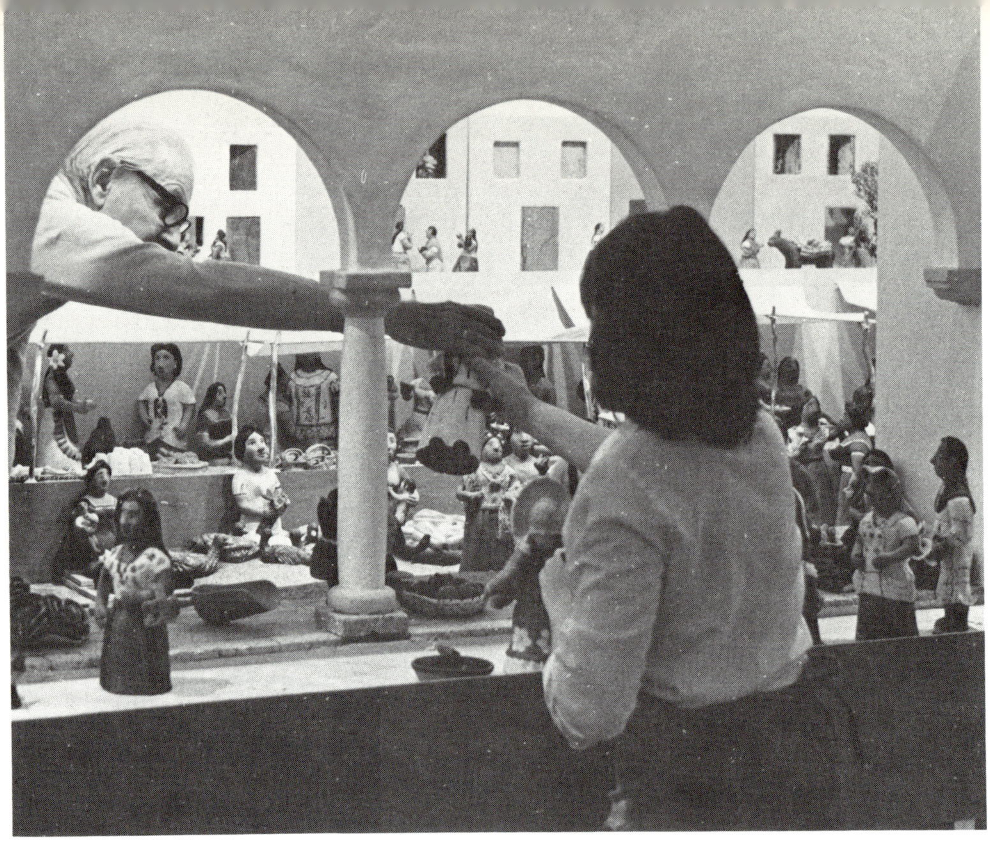

Alexander Girard and Patricia Strong (right) install miniature Ocotlân Mexican village in "Fantasy and Enchantment." Woodcarvings (below) were a major attraction of "Días de Más, Días de Menos."

definition of folk art is difficult to achieve, involving as it does two distinct factors: the producer (folk) and the product (art).

Folk art of particular craftsmen. The unifying theme of several exhibitions has been the *craftsman* rather than his craft. "The New Mexico Santero," 1970-71, emphasized specific craftsmen and illustrated their styles chronologically from the mid-1700s to the present century. Four hundred examples of skin paintings, *retablos* and *bultos* were displayed in authentically reconstructed adobe *nichos*, or wall alcoves. This was one of the most extensive exhibitions ever assembled of northern New Mexico's religious art.

Several exhibitions have displayed the works of contemporary craftsmen. "Patrocino Barela, Woodcarver of Taos, 1900-1964," shown in 1965, included single figures carved in cedar and pine as well as the relief panels for which Barela was best known.

Crafts biennials. Craftspeople working in contemporary and traditional styles have been featured at the Museum's annual juried crafts shows. The first of these was held in 1955, and, with the exception of 1973, the competitions have been organized each year since, although they have been temporarily suspended 1978-82. Originally open to New Mexico artisans only, the shows have alternated since 1965 between the statewide "New Mexico Crafts Biennials" and the regional "Southwest Crafts Biennials," which accept entries from Arizona, Colorado, New Mexico, Oklahoma, Texas, and Utah.

In judging these shows, the jurors, most of whom have been well-known craftsmen themselves, have had to choose objects from an ever-increasing number of entries. In 1963, metalsmiths, potters, weavers, needleworkers, jewelers, and woodworkers submitted 240 entries, from which 71 pieces were chosen for exhibition. By 1977 competition had become far stiffer: 269 artisans submitted 480 entries, 81 of which were selected for the exhibition.

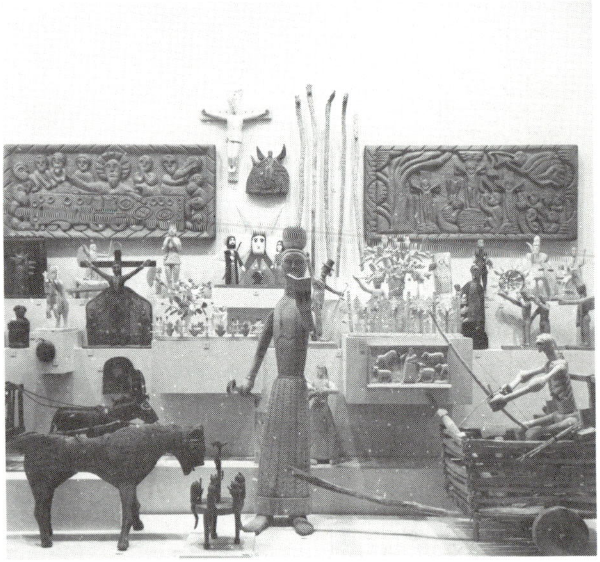

Cash prizes, funded by the International Folk Art Foundation since 1955, have been awarded to especially outstanding craftsmen represented in the biennials. In 1971, these cash awards were supplemented by the opportunity to hold one-month, one-man craft shows at the museum. In other years, the category of Purchase Award was added to the cash prizes, with MOIFA buying the pieces selected for its own collections. All of these awards, plus the yearly Honorable Mentions, have paid tribute to top craftspeople and indicate that excellent workmanship and quality design are indeed still alive.

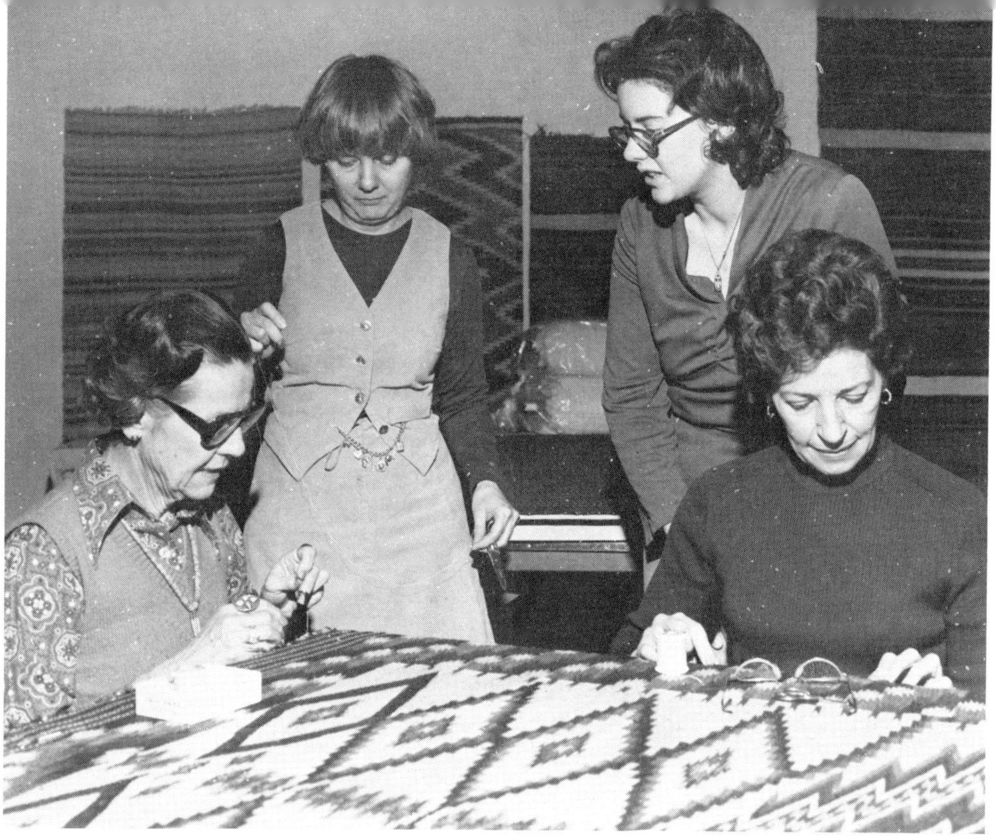

Jean Cartwright, Nora Pickens, Charlotte Mitchell and Mary Hall (left) mount textiles for "Spanish Textile Tradition of New Mexico and Colorado." Display below is from 1977 Southwest Crafts Biennial.

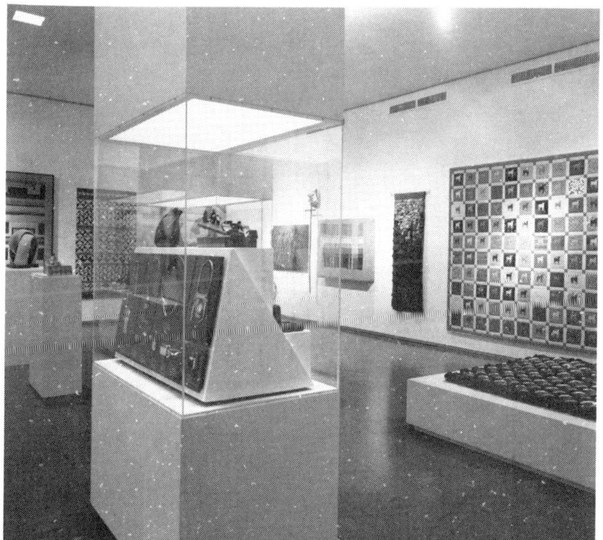

SPECIAL PROGRAMS

Although exhibitions have received increased attention lately, they have never been the only means by which the museum has reached its audience. Programs have been particularly numerous, with crafts demonstrations, films, folk dances, musical performances, puppet shows, and lectures all having contributed toward making the museum a "place for activity rather than simply for exhibition galleries," as envisioned by Miss Bartlett.

Typical of the crafts demonstrations that MOIFA has frequently sponsored are those that were held during 1968. In the spring of that year the Mondragon family of woodcarvers from Cordova, New Mexico, gave a demonstration of their art in conjunction with the exhibition, "Folk Art in Wood." Later that year, four artisans were invited to demonstrate the techniques used in production of the crafts they exhibited in the "1968 New Mexico Craftsmen's Exhibition." Blue Corn of San Ildefonso demonstrated the traditional Indian coil method of making pottery, while Cynthia Homire threw pots on a modern electric wheel. Rachel Brown showed onlookers how to spin, while Mike Selig wove, both on and off the loom, incorporating various non-fiber materials into his fabric.

The idea of demonstration was elaborated into a series of innovative Textile Workshops sponsored by the International Folk Art Foundation and held at the museum in 1972, 1973 and 1974. Aspiring crafts workers were able to participate in the actual processes, not merely to observe them. Under the direction of well-known crafts teachers, students developed their skills in such fields as embroidery, vegetable dyeing, macrame, patchwork, card weaving, loom weaving, and off-loom fabric construction. The Textile Workshops eventually became so successful that they outgrew the museum's facilities and were able to find more diversified funding.

The film library has grown to include around a hundred films, all documenting folklife and art. These, as well as rented films, have been shown at festivals and series regularly scheduled in the museum's auditorium. A few of these, of course, have won a special place in the calendar: *And Now Miguel,* a story about sheepherding life in New Mexico's Sangre de Cristo Mountains, has been shown annually since 1963, and *Day of the Dead,* a study of All Souls' Day as celebrated in Mexico, has likewise become standard fare.

In addition to film showings, the auditorium has been the scene of numerous folk dance, music and song

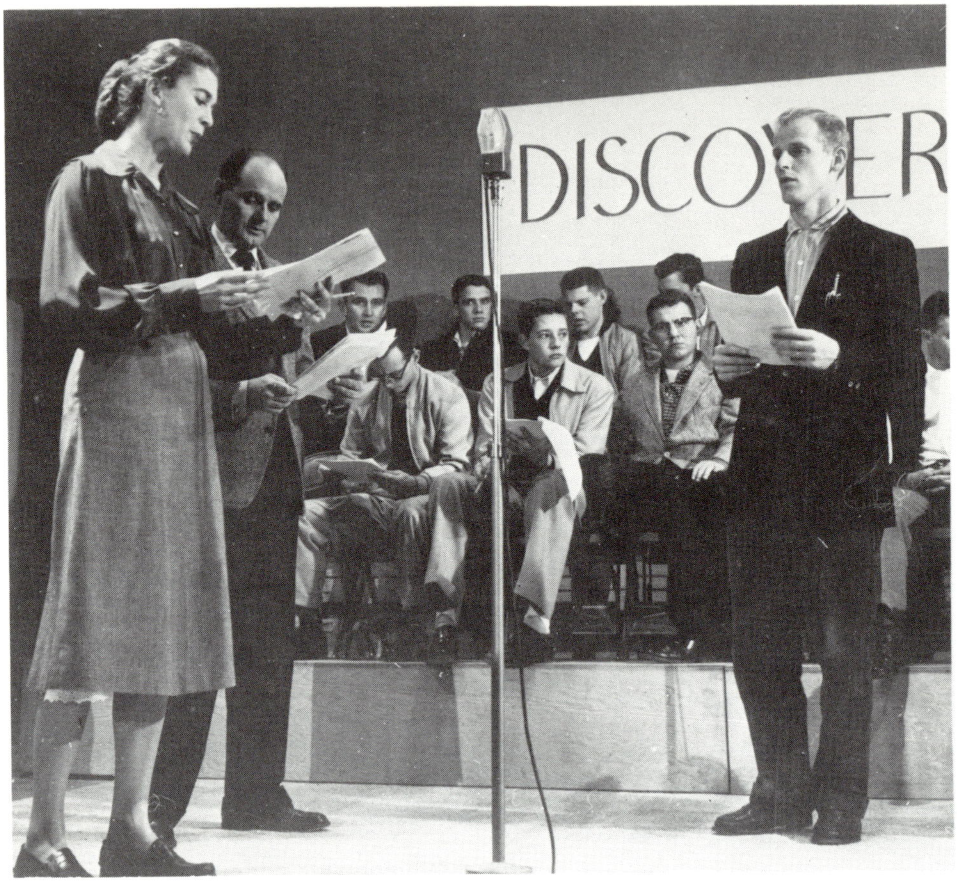

On stage at "Discovery" radio program, created and produced by the Museum of International Folk Art in the early 1950s.

presentations. Performers have come from as far away as Korea and Japan, yet the museum has drawn upon close-at-hand talent as well, with programs of Pueblo Indian and Spanish dance and music.

The auditorium has also been used from time to time for Foundation sponsored lectures and panel discussions, although just a handful have been held in recent years. Distinguished speakers have included Dr. Wayland D. Hand, director of the Center for the Study of Comparative Folklore and Mythology at UCLA, who spoke on Chilean folk art; Albert Eskeröd, chief curator of the Nordiska Museet in Stockholm, giving an illustrated lecture on Swedish wall paintings; Dr. Merle G. Wachter, chairman of the Art Center, University of the Americas, who spoke on contemporary popular arts of Mexico; Dr. Yedida K. Stillman, of the State University of New York in Binghamton, with a discussion of Palestinian costumes; Dr. Heinz Edgar Kiewe, author of *History of Folk Cross Stitch,* who brought slides and fabric samples to enrich his lecture, "Folk Embroideries of the Mediterranean"; folklorist Michael Owen Jones, who discussed a special Kentucky chair maker, Chester Cornett, in his lecture, "He Kin Make a Chair so Purty You Kin See Yore Face Shinin' in It: Some Reflections on Folk Aesthetics"; and musicologist Dr. John D. Robb of the University of New Mexico, speaking on the folk music of New Mexico.

Until 1978, when it was closed down to provide space for Girard Foundation Collection processing, the auditorium was in frequent use by community organizations. Folk dance groups practiced regularly there for several years; ballet groups scheduled dance films; and museum and archaeological organizations found it a congenial place for their meetings. The most popular event, however, has long been the January performance of the old Spanish play, *Los Tres Reyes Magos* (The Three Kings). Produced each year since 1962 by the Cabelleros de Vargas organization with assistance from the Sociedad Folklórica, this drama employs a script based in large part on the traditional presentation at Taos. The play impresses modern audiences as much as it once affected Spanish colonists of the eighteenth and nineteenth centuries.

EXTENSION ACTIVITIES

Over the years the museum's services have reached beyond its walls on Camino Lejo through many different extension programs. Certainly the best known of these has been the traveling exhibition service. Beginning in 1956 (and funded by the International

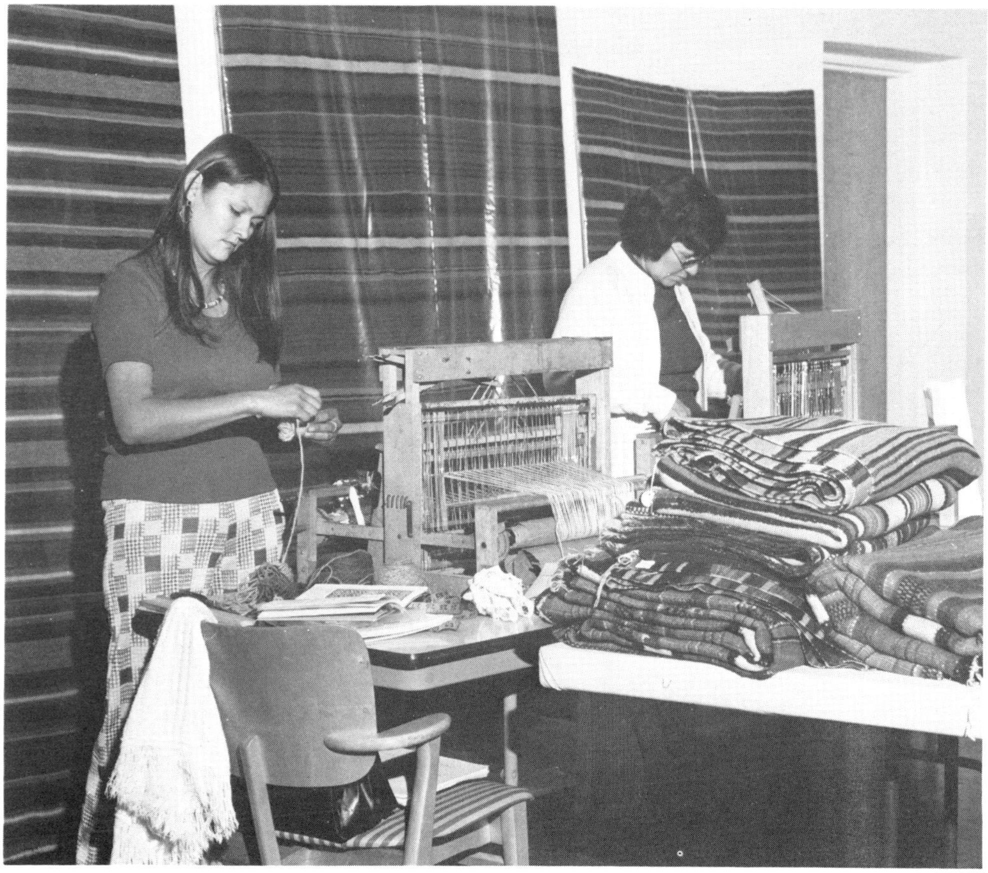

Ellen Arellano and Anita Martinez prepare looms for weaving at the Rio Grande Weaving and Dyeing Workshops held in 1976.

Folk Art Foundation through 1970) a semi-trailer van carried twelve self-contained folk art exhibits over the state to several thousand elementary school children in public, parochial and Bureau of Indian Affairs schools. Before the van rolled into town each year, teaching aids were sent to the local schools so that teachers could discuss the content of the exhibition with their students. When it actually arrived, the driver-curator guided youngsters through such shows as "Tools and Wood-Working in Spanish New Mexico" and "Climate of Man's Living," a comparison of human adaptations to arctic and tropical climates.

The success of the children's traveling unit led to establishment of an adult unit in 1964-65. "The Idea of Folk Art," comprised of artifacts from the Florence Dibell Bartlett Collection, was the first of several adult units to be van transported and set up at various community centers throughout the state. Subsequent units, such as "Mountain Folk of the Southern Appalachians" and "Durable Metal: Timeless Art," were accompanied by films, catalogs and photographs. In 1971 the Museum of New Mexico assumed full ownership of these units, with responsibility for their operation being transferred from MOIFA to the Education Bureau of the Museum.

A radio program, *"Discovery,"* acquainted many area residents with the museum during the first years of its existence. Each segment dramatized a folk tale or legend from a different part of the world. Since its discontinuation in the mid-1950s, the museum has not produced broadcast programs itself, but its director and curators have frequently made guest appearances on radio and television shows.

Loans of collection materials to other museums have also played an important role in MOIFA's attempts to reach a wider audience. Every year the museum receives at least a score of requests for objects ranging from bultos to wooden bears. These are given favorable attention in almost every instance. Recently the museum also circulated two complete exhibitions, "Navajo Pictorial Weaving" and "African Fabrics from the Girard Foundation Collection," to other museums, and a third, "Spanish Textile Tradition of New Mexico and Colorado," is scheduled to travel to both the Smithsonian Institution and the American Museum of Natural History.

Alarmed at the rising number of thefts of New Mexican religious art, the museum launched in 1973 a photographic inventory of religious objects in northern New Mexico churches, chapels and other sites. The

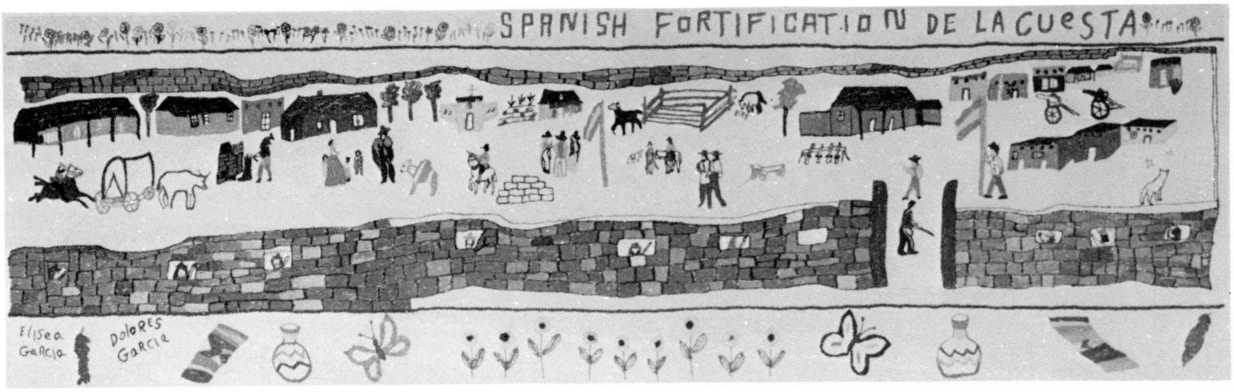

Women of the village of Villanueva fashioned a Bicentennial tapestry under MOIFA sponsorship. Archbishop Roberto Sanchez dedicated the several panels at Villanueva's church in July, 1976.

project, aimed at forestalling such losses, received strong financial support from the National Endowment for the Arts, the New Mexico Arts Commission, the New Mexico State Planning Office, and the International Folk Art Foundation.

TEACHING PROJECTS

Most direct of all the extension services, however, have been the extended teaching projects. The first of these, "Village Workshops in Embroidery," 1973-74, was funded by the International Folk Art Foundation and involved women of the New Mexico villages of Pecos, Medanales, La Madera, Santa Cruz, Villanueva, and Guadalupita. During both summers they were instructed in the techniques of embroidery by Carmen Benavente de Orrego-Salas, noted for her success with a similar project in Ninhue, Chile. At the end of the second summer, the museum held an exhibition of these women's completed work—several small embroidered scenes and three large pictorial quilts.

An outgrowth of this experiment's success was the Villanueva Tapestry project. Under MOIFA's sponsorship, the women of that village received a National Endowment for the Arts grant for a unique Bicentennial undertaking: embroidery of Villanueva's history in a "tapestry." By early spring of 1976 they had completed 265 feet of pictorial embroidery on linen backing. All this was permanently installed at the parish church in Villaneuva and was dedicated in July 1976 amidst great ceremony. This singular work continues to attract occasional visitors to Villanueva, to be sure, but more important, it showed the village women that they possess a great deal of creative ability. A totally unexpected side benefit, the women observed with real satisfaction, was that the project also brought them closer together than they had been before—even in a village as small as Villanueva.

As the Villanueva project drew to a successful close, the museum was planning its next set of teaching sessions. Interested weavers from the northern mountains and valleys were invited to the two three-day sessions of the Rio Grande Weaving and Dyeing Workshop in September and October 1976. Participants, working alongside MOIFA staff members, dyed skein after skein of wool with native plant dyes and other traditional dyes known to Spanish weavers of a century ago.

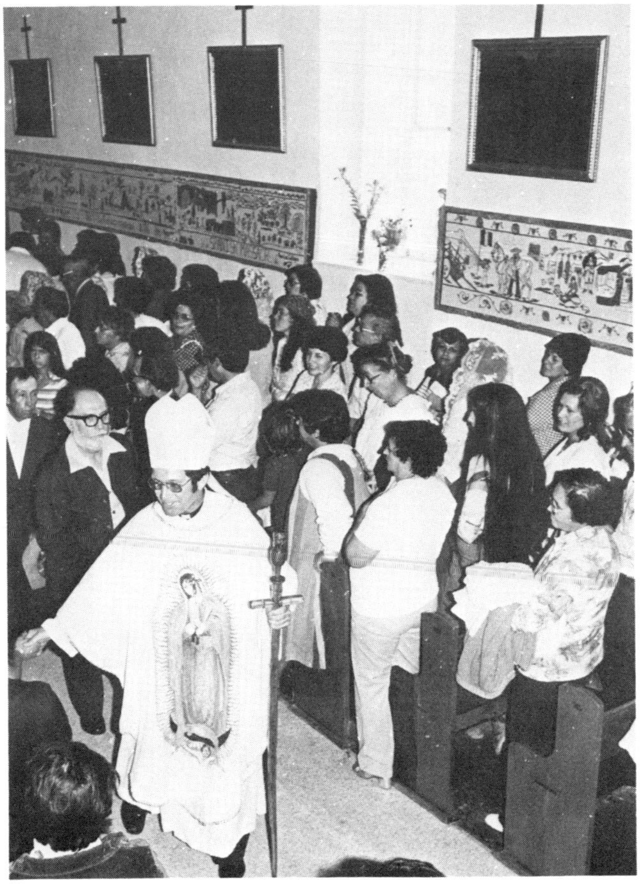

They spent additional time analyzing design elements and use of color in dozens of old Rio Grande weavings from the museum's collections and then, using the wool they themselves had dyed, produced small weavings of their own. This project, funded by a grant from the New Mexico Arts Commission, made weavers more aware of their fine local Spanish weaving traditions and helped them design weavings that bring better market prices.

RESEARCH AND PUBLICATIONS

Scarcely a day has passed at the museum when staff members have not performed research of one sort or another. Most frequently they are concerned simply with gathering enough information on some newly acquired object to fill out an accession sheet. Often they are preparing for an exhibition and are engaged in more extensive study, poring over library materials and contacting specialists in an effort to arrive at accurate conclusions about their material. They summarize their findings in the show's label text and sometimes in a checklist as well; on nearly fifty occasions staffers have produced a small catalog to accompany the exhibition.

Some research efforts, however, have been of far greater magnitude and have resulted in complete books and monographs. Both research and publication costs in these instances have usually been backed by the International Folk Art Foundation.

Earliest of such studies was Laura Gilpin's ambitious project to photograph both Maya ruins and contemporary Indian villages in Central America. These efforts formed the basis for her book, *Folk Art of Yucatan*, which appeared in 1961, and an exhibition by the same title.

At this same time, E. Boyd was well into the pioneer studies that have made her name synonymous with Spanish Colonial art. She turned out several smaller catalogs and handbooks at the museum, including *Popular Arts of Colonial New Mexico* (1959), *Santos: How to Name Them* (1966), and *The New Mexico Santero* (1969), before finishing her major effort, *Popular Arts of Spanish New Mexico* (1974). This last work, summarizing a lifetime of study, is probably the single most important publication to date on the Spanish Colonial art of New Mexico.

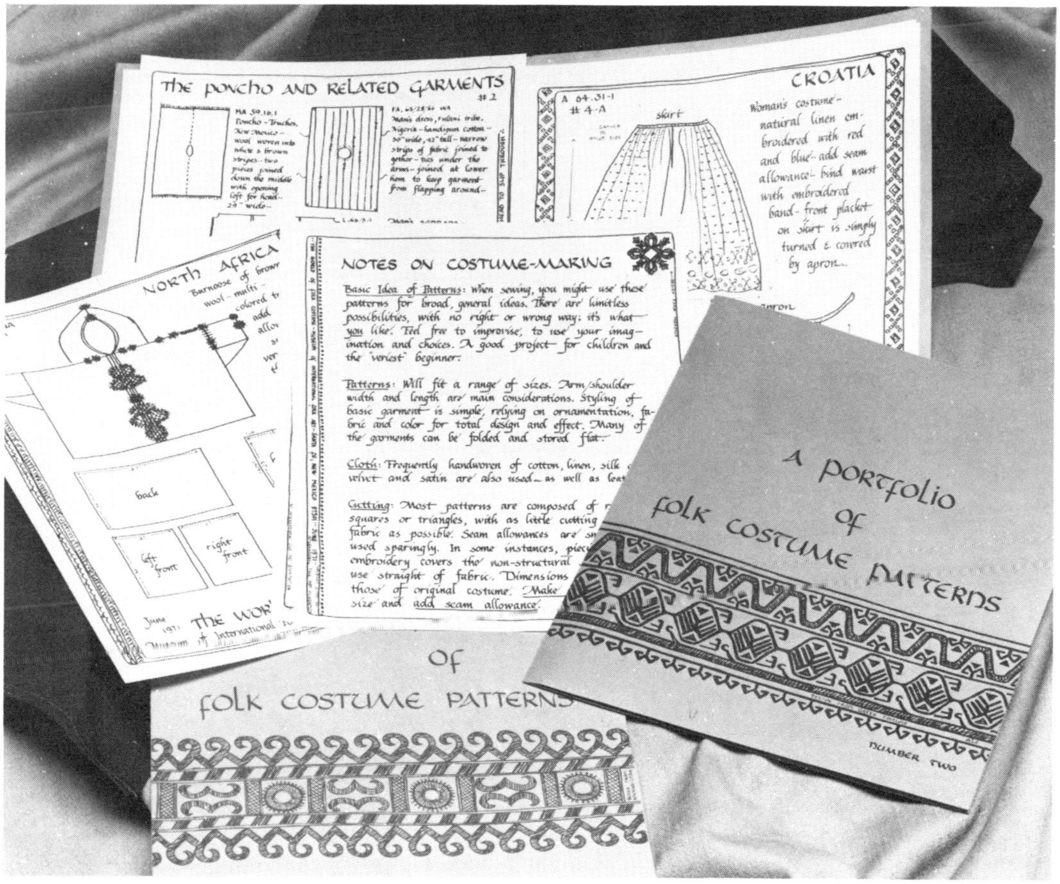

Exquisite folk costume portfolios were produced by IFAF, MOIFA and the Museum Press.

Still other studies have also dealt with Spanish Colonial life and art. An enormous project involving folk drama, music and dance required years of data collection and analysis by curator Richard Stark and research associate Frank Bond. Stark's studies have resulted in *Music of the Spanish Folk Plays in New Mexico* (1969), and *Juegos Infantiles* (1973); other publications by Bond as well as Stark are still in progress.

Leona Davis Boylan's research on MOIFA's holdings of Spanish Colonial silver, as well as those of other institutions, led to publication of *Spanish Colonial Silver* by the Museum of New Mexico Press in 1975. The following year, Robert H. and Florence Lister received a similar grant from the International Folk Art Foundation to study the museum's fine majolica collection. Publication of their resulting manuscript is anticipated.

Costumes, too, have been the subject of recent studies. In 1971, two *Portfolios of Folk Costume Patterns* appeared in conjunction with the "World of Folk Costume" exhibition. These portfolios of patterns and embroidery were novel in two respects: they were prepared by unpaid volunteers, working under the direction of curator Carol Steiro, and they represented some of the first efforts at pattern analysis of folk costume in this country. They remain best-sellers even today.

In 1972-74 Yedida K. Stillman researched the large collection of Palestinian costumes owned by the Foundation and the museum. Her work led to the exhibition, "More Splendid than the Shining Full Moon: Costumes

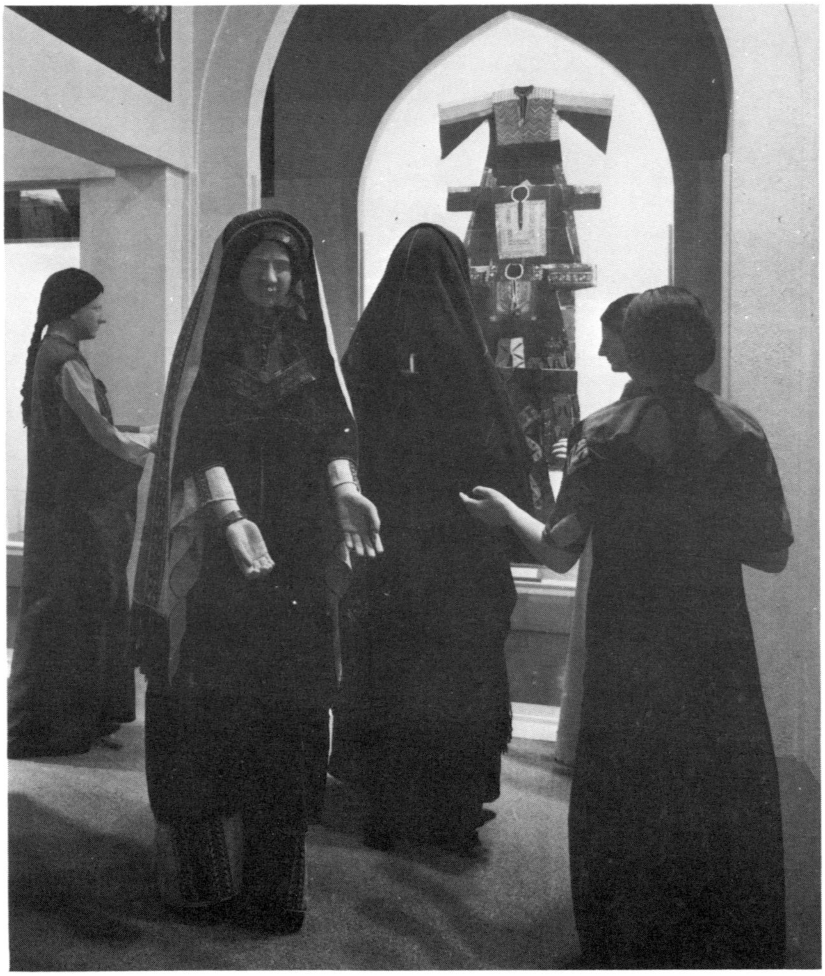

"More Splendid than the Shining Full Moon," (1977-79) displayed the colorful folk costumes of the Arabs of Palestine.

from Old Palestine," a feature article in EL PALACIO (Winter 1977), and the publication of her book, *Palestinian Costumes and Jewelry* (1978).

Another extended study of costumes involved the Mixtec Indian garments from Mexico. Nancy Byers Roberts worked from 1976 through 1978 on this project, which may also result in an exhibition and a publication.

An undertaking that rivaled the Spanish Colonial folk music and drama project in complexity was the recent study of Southwest Spanish textiles. In 1967 curator E. Boyd mapped out the original objectives: to gather information on Spanish weavings and to compile a list of the holdings of this type in museums of the United States. By 1969 research associate Dorothy B. Bowen had examined and recorded information about 1,100 textiles to complete this phase of the project. The project resumed again in 1975 when it adopted four new goals: to study ten additional collections; to analyze the dyes used in the textiles; to organize an exhibition illustrating the project's conclusions; and, finally, to publish a catalog of the findings including not only the technical elements of the weavings, but also the historical, social and economic aspects of their manufacture and use. The National Endowment for the Arts and the International Folk Art Foundation agreed to fund this project. Coordinated by curator Nora Fisher, it came to involve the efforts of nearly a dozen specialists. The exhibition, "Spanish Textile Tradition of New Mexico and Colorado," opened in mid-1978, and an impressive book bearing the same title is on the current list from the Museum of New Mexico Press.

Despite the relatively small size of its staff and the heavy workload each member carries, the museum will undoubtedly continue to value staff research projects, for the studies completed over the past twenty-five years have indeed contributed much of value to the fields of folk art and folklife.

THE VISITORS TO MOIFA

Attendance records show that the annual number of visitors has risen steadily through the years, attaining in excess of 80,000 recorded visits in 1976 and 1977. The Museum of International Folk Art draws people of all ages and tour groups not only from New Mexico and the Southwest but also from across the country, neighboring Canada and Mexico, and abroad. It is not uncommon during the summer to have chartered buses disgorge tourists from France, Germany, Belgium, Japan, and other foreign lands. These visitors nearly always express surprise and delight upon finding exhibitions that reflect the museum's truly international scope. This, no doubt, would have pleased Florence Dibell Bartlett immensely!

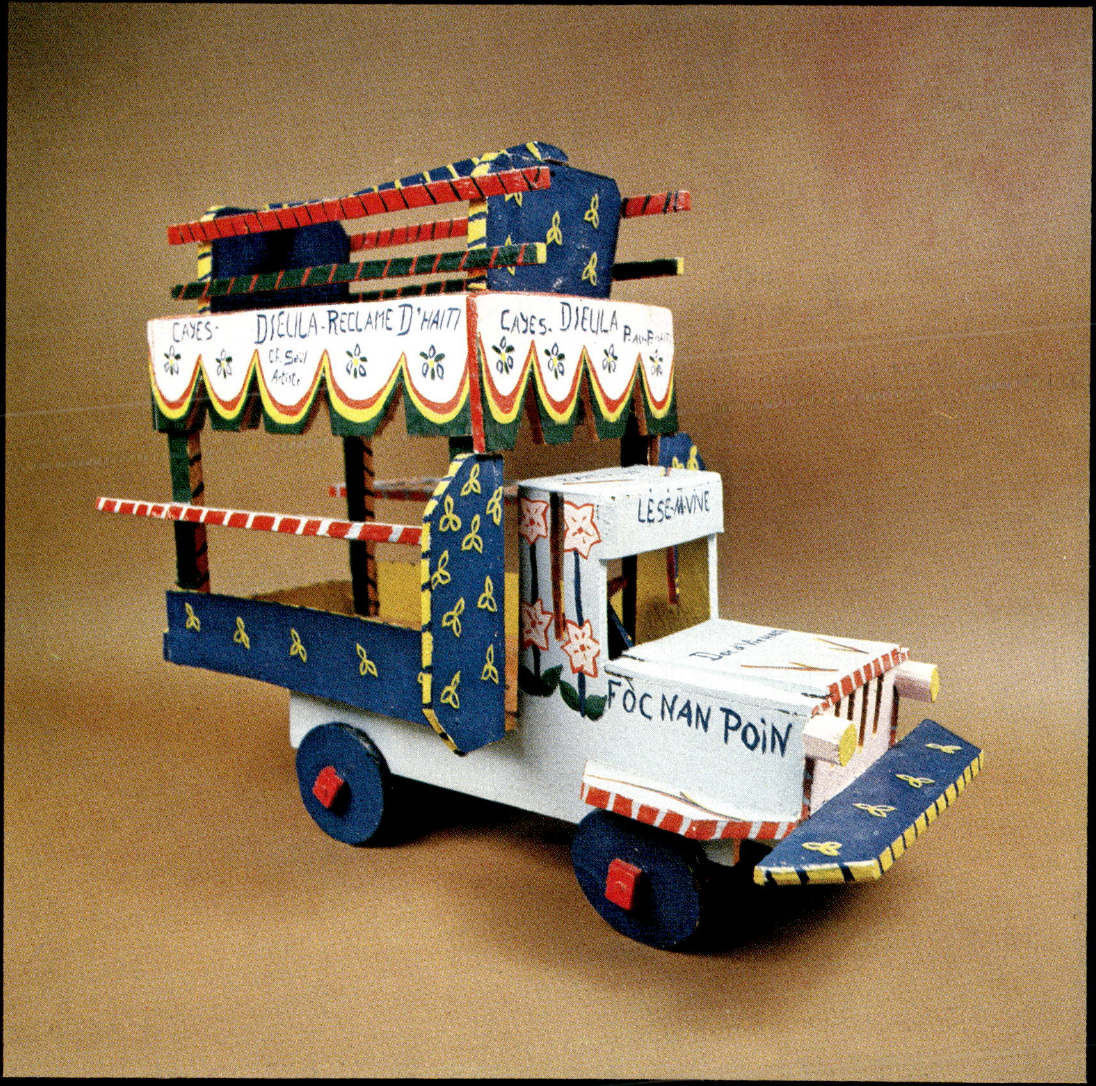

Bus ("Camion") from Haiti (65 cm. long). From the International Folk Art Foundation Collection.

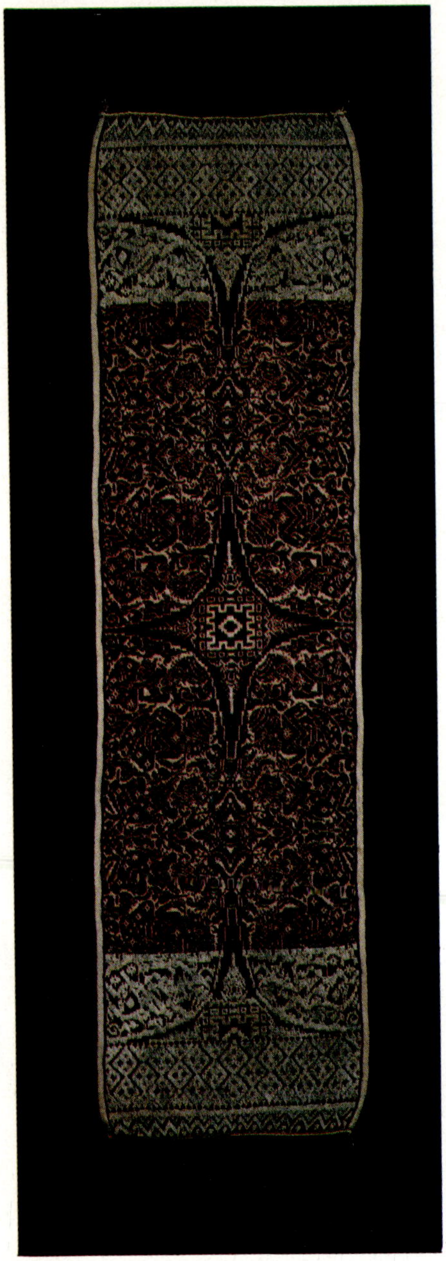

Left: Shoulder cloth ("Kain Geringsing") from Tenganan, Bali, late nineteenth century (2 m. long). From the Miss C. F. Bieber Collection in the International Folk Art Foundation Collection.

Below: Majolica pot ("Orza") from Puente del Arzobispo, Spain, 1680-1725 (17.3 cm. high). Gift of William Ilfeld.

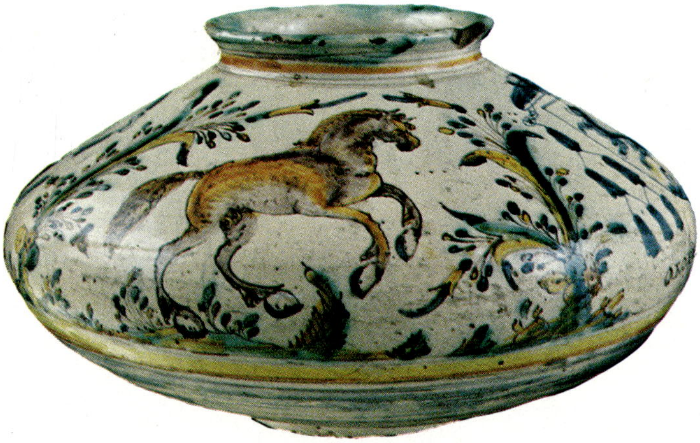

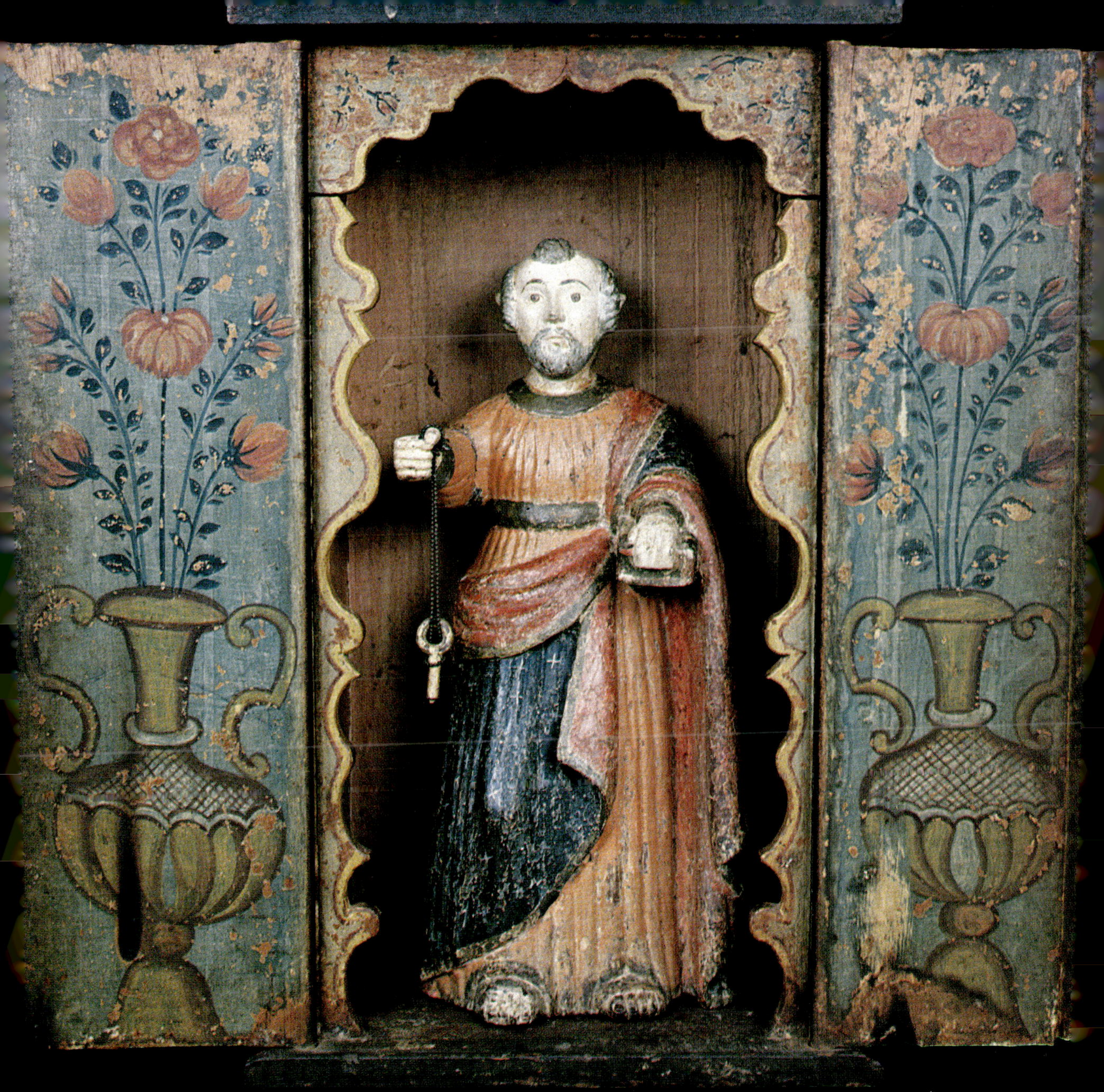

St. Peter in niche, made in Paraguay in the eighteenth or nineteenth century (68 cm. high). The statue is a gift of Paul N. Wenger; the niche is part of the E. Boyd Memorial Fund, International Folk Art Foundation Collection.

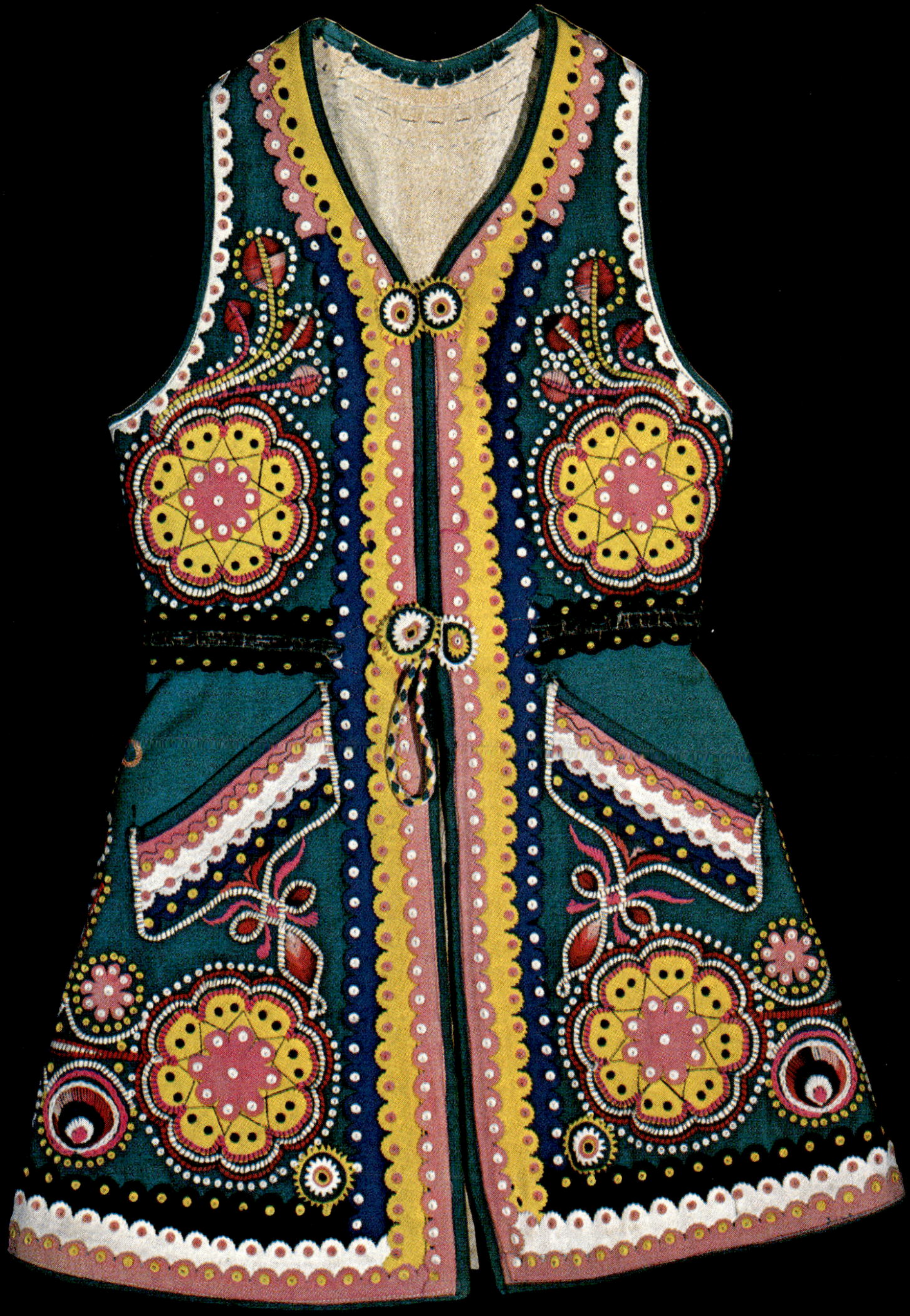

Appliquéd woman's coat from Zagreb, Yugoslavia, twentieth century (76 cm. long). Gift of Florence Dibell Bartlett.

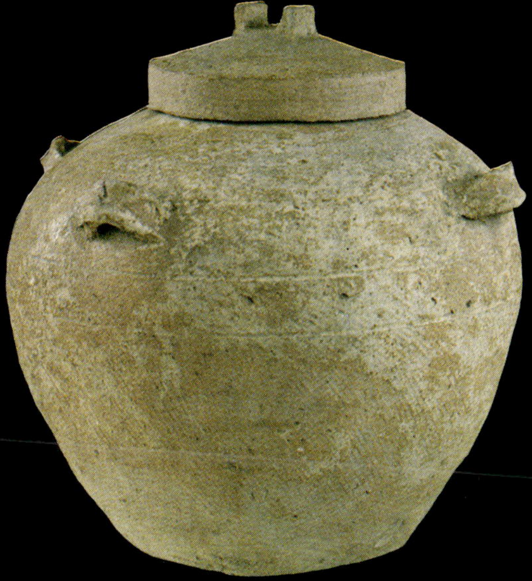

Photograph by Art Taylor

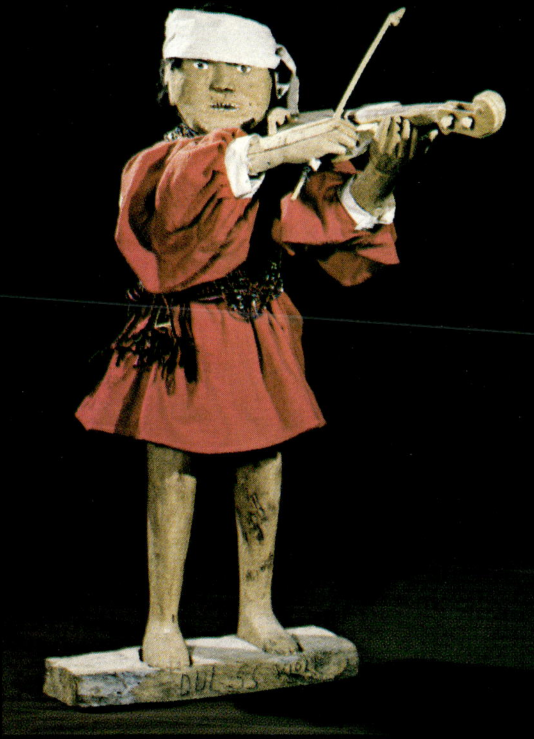

Above: Japanese jar with lid, from Nara Period 645-796 AD (29 cm. high). International Folk Art Foundation Collection.

Right: Violin player, made by the Tarahumara people of Batopilas Canyon, Chihuahua, Mexico, 1978 (90 cm. high).

Below: Hooked rug from York, Pennsylvania, circa 1890 (108 cm. long). International Folk Art Foundation Collection.

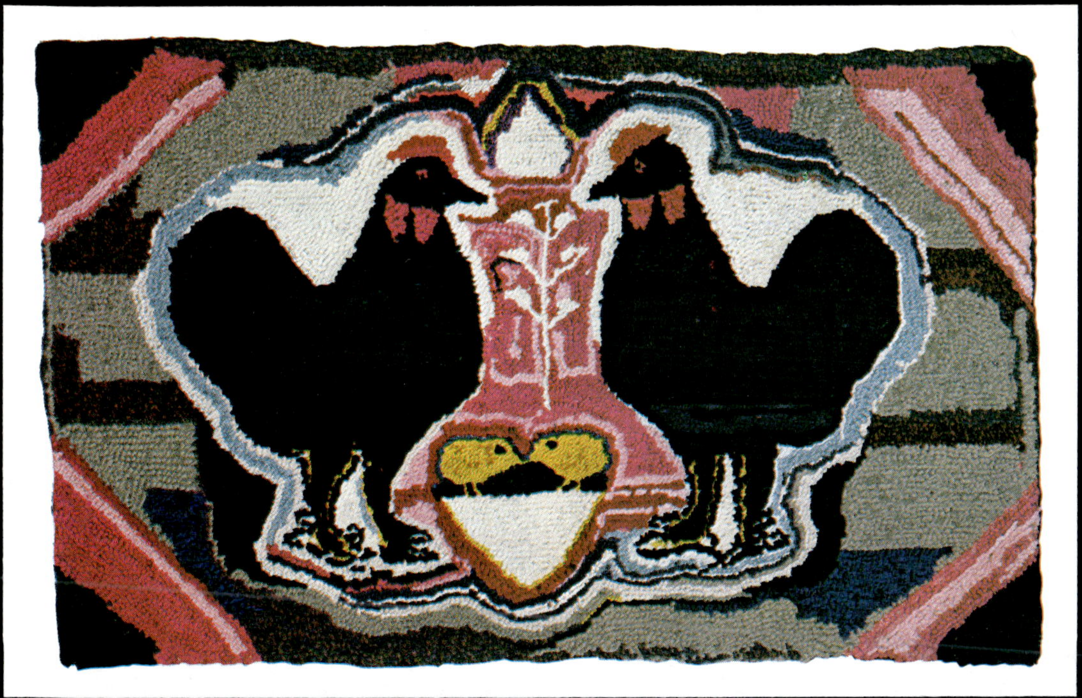

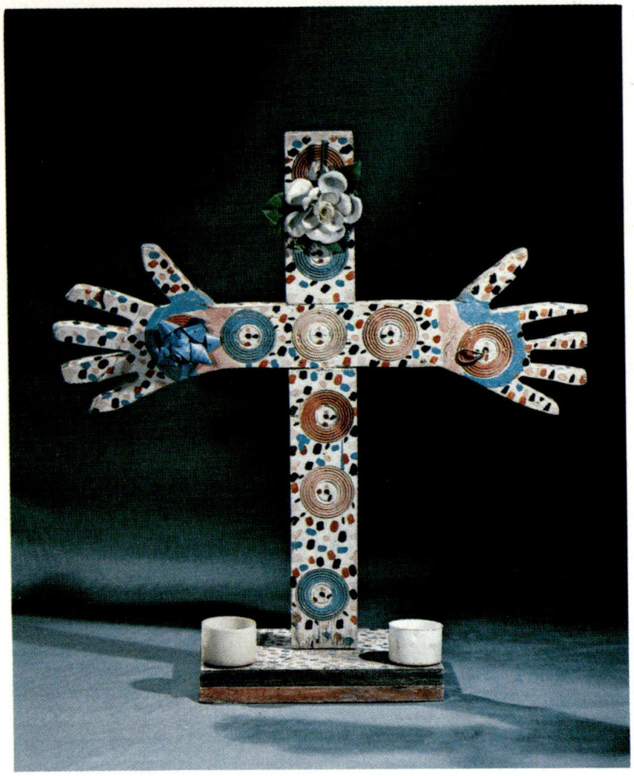

Cross made by Paul Pacheco of Española, New Mexico, circa 1945 (64 cm. high). Purchased with the aid of funds from the National Endowment for the Arts and the International Folk Art Foundation.

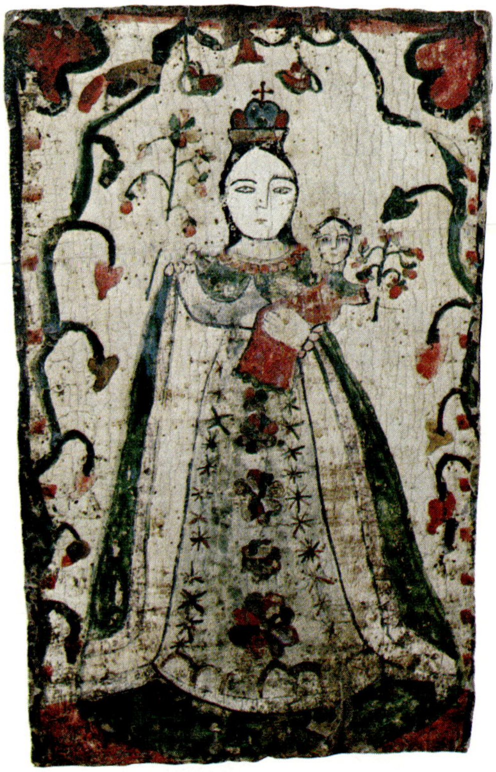

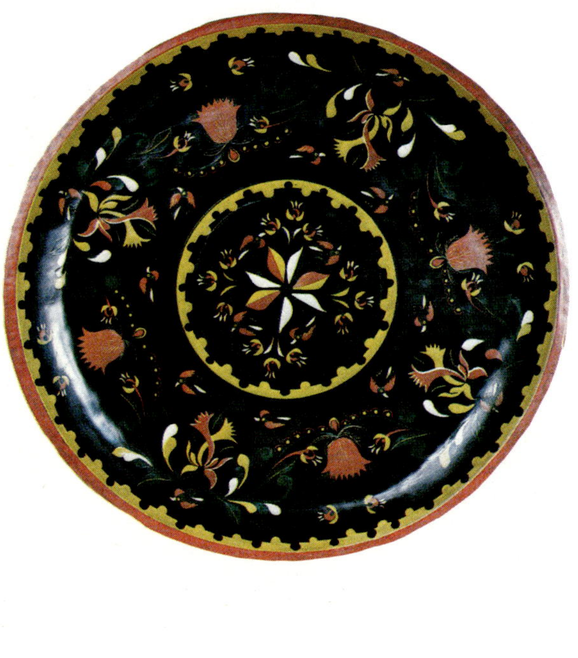

Above: Virgin and Child ("La Virgen con El Niño") from northern New Mexico, circa 1850 (31 cm. high). A bequest of Mary Austin.

Left: Lacquered tray ("Batea") from Uruapan, Michoacan, Mexico, circa 1920 (52 cm. diameter). Gift from the René d'Harnoncourt Collection.

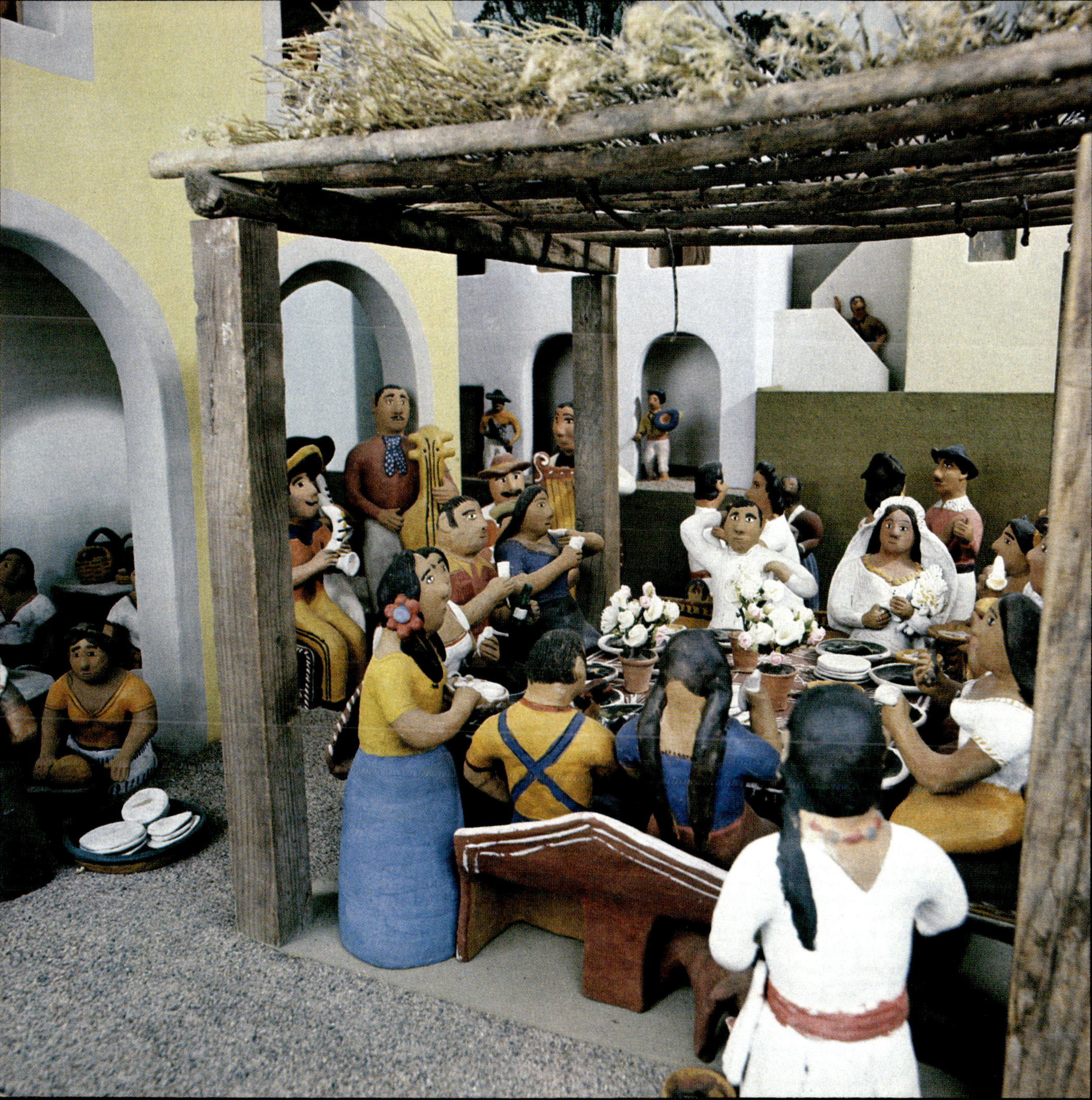

Wedding scene, made by the Aguilar family of Ocotlán, Oaxaca, Mexico.
From the exhibition, "Fantasy and Enchantment: Selections from the Girard Foundation Collection."

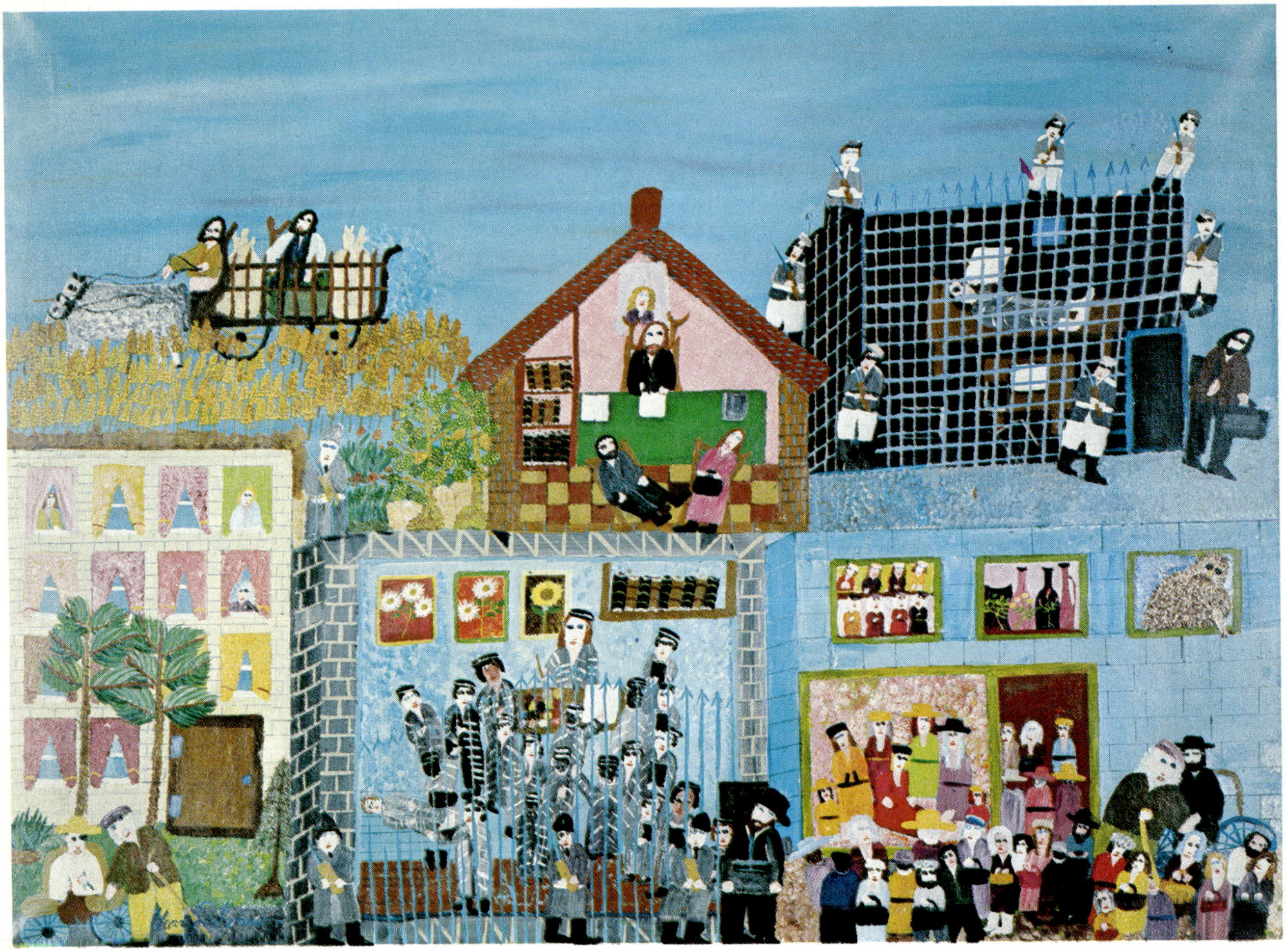

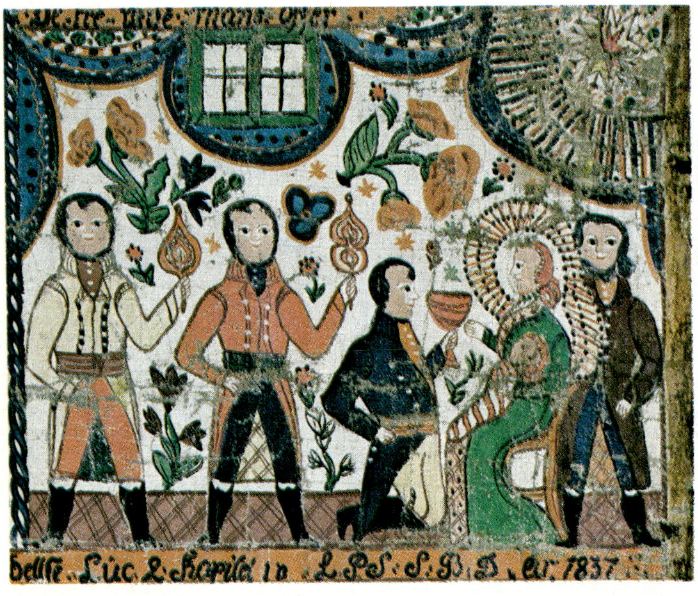

Above: "The Mystique of Life," painted by Harry Lieberman of Great Neck, New York, 1972 (78 cm. x 103 cm.). The canvas illustrates the artist's philosophy of life through six vignettes: through hope and will, people overcome their circumstances, help others, and survive spiritually.

Left: Detail of Christmas wall hanging from Smaland, Sweden, 1832. International Folk Art Foundation Collection (see cover).

EXPLORING MOIFA'S MAGNIFICENT COLLECTIONS

By Laura Byers

1978 Summer Intern at the Museum of International Folk Art

SINCE ITS INAUGURATION, the collections housed at the Museum of International Folk Art have increased from the original 2,500 objects given by the museum's founder, Florence Bartlett, to a total of some 19,000 items.

Few visitors have the opportunity to see the full extent and variety of the museum's holdings. Exhibitions can only hint at the size and scope of the accumulation, which features a worldwide selection of costumes, jewelry, figurative ceramics, and nativities; European household and decorative art; Spanish Colonial religious art; and silver, ceramics, furniture and textiles.

The types of objects acquired have in part been determined by the contents of Miss Bartlett's original gift. Shortages of time, space and money are the collector's opponents, and early in the museum's history it became apparent that these factors would limit purchasing. As it was impossible to represent every distinctive region of the world equally well, and unwise to compete with or duplicate the holdings of other institutions, the Folk Art Museum committed itself to a policy of building solidly on the strengths of the collections it already owned.

Costumes and their accompanying jewelry from around the world dominated Florence Dibell Bartlett's original gift to the museum. From this nucleus there developed in time a costume collection that rivals and occasionally surpasses leading costume holdings elsewhere in the world. Particularly noteworthy are Miss Bartlett's Scandinavian and domestic textiles.

The museum owes thanks to Santa Fe resident Miss C. F. Bieber, among others, for the quality of its Asian costume and textile collection. Miss Bieber's gifts include Chinese, Indian, and Indonesian articles which have been supplemented by recent acquisitions from Tibet and the Kutch area of India.

The Palestinian costume collection, recently the subject of a major exhibit at MOIFA, was begun by Florence Dibell Bartlett and

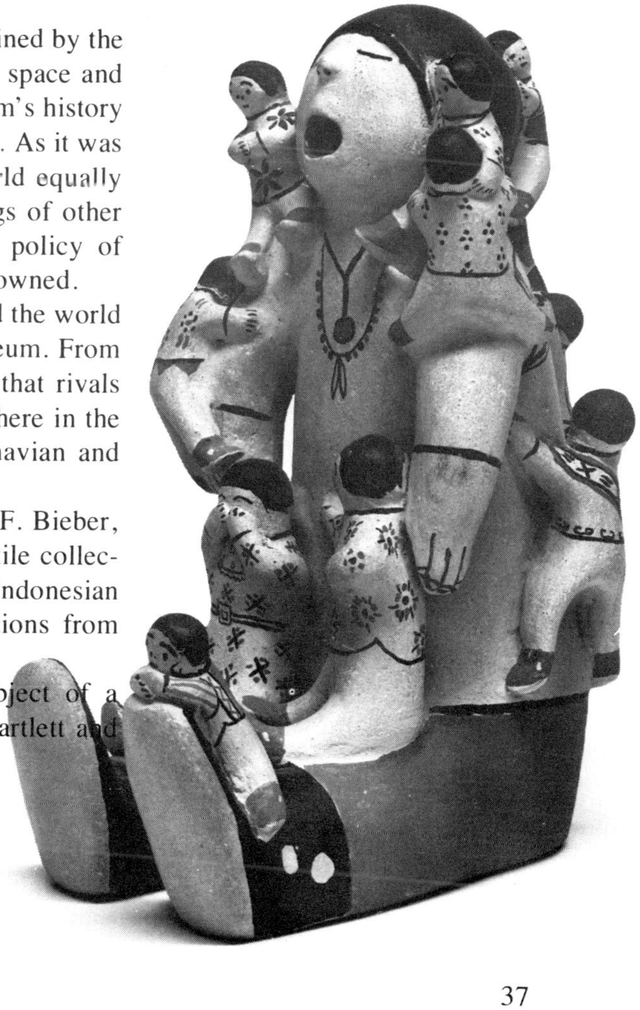

Popular "storyteller" figure by Helen Cordero of Cochiti Pueblo, New Mexico. A gift of Sallie Wagner to the International Folk Art Foundation Collection, the figure measures 27 cm. high.

augmented by a sizeable purchase from Mrs. Widad Kawar of the Kingdom of Jordan. Most impressive of the costumes in this group are the wedding garments and apparel from Bethlehem and Ramallah in Judea.

What really distinguishes ethnic costume, besides the skillfulness of its construction, is the imaginative freedom of design, color and texture it frequently displays. The dazzling array of Indian costumes from Mexico and Central America are among the museum's most cherished possessions. The Shook Collection of Guatemalan costumes was acquired in 1971. The Mexican Indian costume collection, representing twenty-four tribal groups, is composed of garments from Miss Bartlett's original gift, the Elizabeth Norman bequest, and the Donald Cordry Collection acquired by the International Folk Art Foundation.

Accessories—particularly hats, shoes, and jewelry—complete the costumes. The Mexican Indian garments, for instance, are matched with a complete assortment of Mexican Indian jewelry. A superb array of Araucanian silver, the bequest of Edith Page Skewes-Cox, represents the Mapuche Indians of central Chile and Argentina. In contrast to the bold styling of the Araucanian jewelry is the museum's international assemblage of delicately crafted filigree jewelry. A representative assortment of New Mexican filigree from the J. C. Candelario store was a gift from Mr. and Mrs. W. J. Wilson.

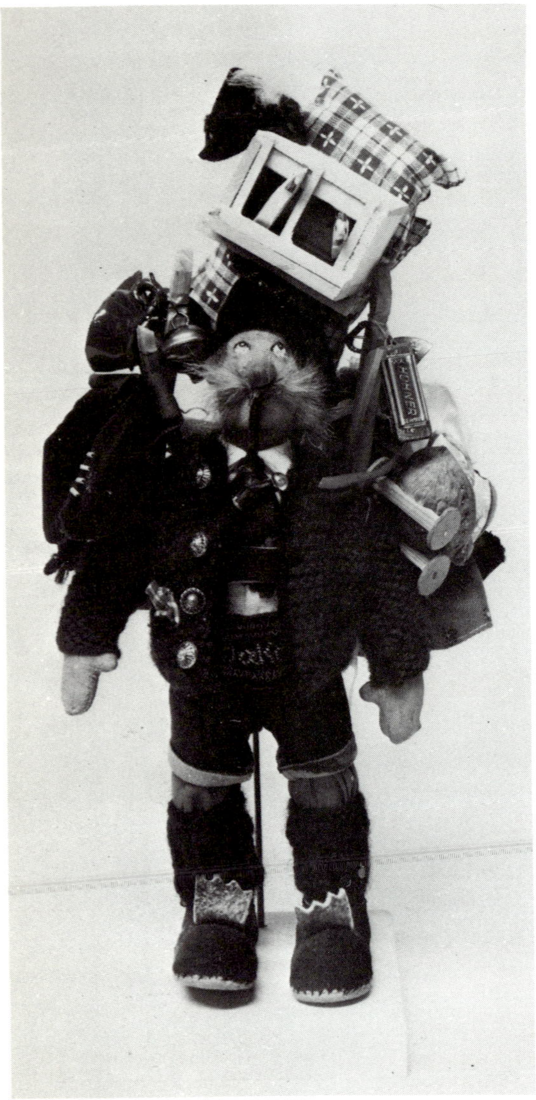

"Cheap Jack" doll (above and opposite page) comes from Saltzburg, Austria. A gift of Dr. J. Monroe Thorington to the IFAF Collection (33 cm. high).

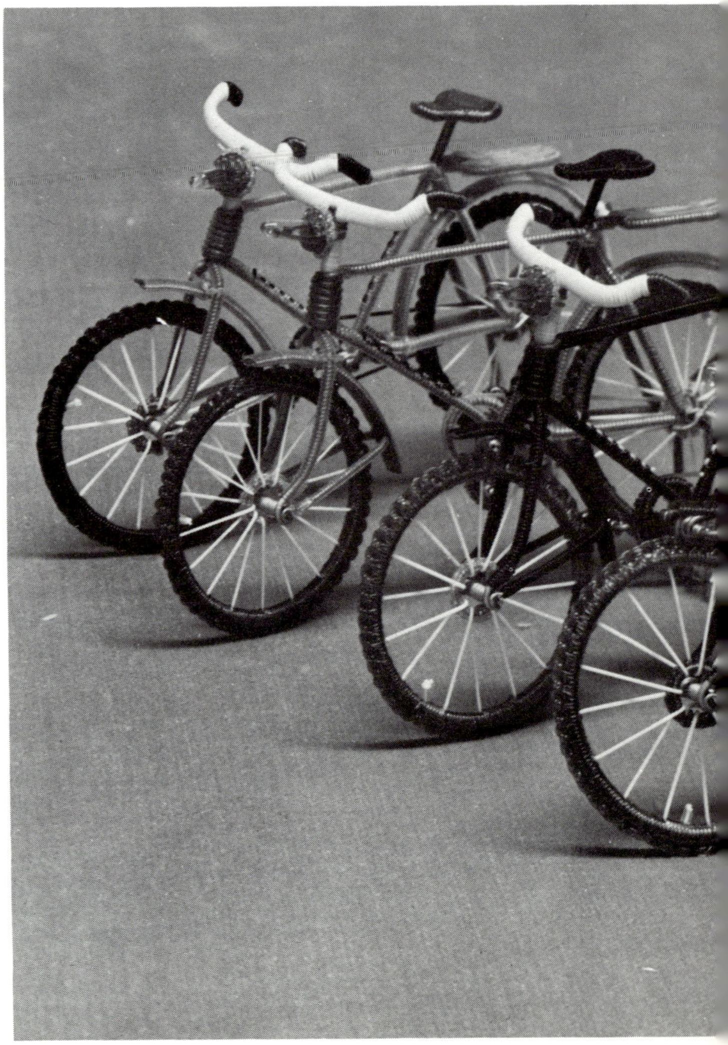

In 1962 the museum was pleasantly surprised by International Business Machines' gift of nineteen pieces of South American silver. These items, in conjunction with other gifts and purchases by the International Folk Art Foundation, enhance the colonial silver accumulation from Argentina, Bolivia, Guatemala, Mexico and Peru.

Two major textile collections reflect different aspects of MOIFA's collection policy. The *ikat* (fabric woven of yarn that has been tied and dyed) collection is a truly international gathering selected on the basis of technique and medium. The museum's quilts and coverlets from eastern and central North America, while also united by technique, strongly emphasize a regional craft tradition. This relatively small but choice collection was given by Gertrude Clarke and several other donors.

Today, it is recognized that the early Spanish settlers along the Rio Grande introduced weavings with stylistic features distinct from those of the Indian weavers of the Southwest. The museum has quite a number of Rio Grande blankets that exemplify this separate tradition, thanks to many donors, including Alfred I. Barton, Mrs. Hatton L. Clark, Mr. and Mrs. John Gaw Meem, Mary L. M. Peck, Mrs. Edgar L. Rossin, and the Historical Society of New Mexico.

The museum's holdings in New Mexican religious art provide an important emotional and historical focus for the Spanish surnamed

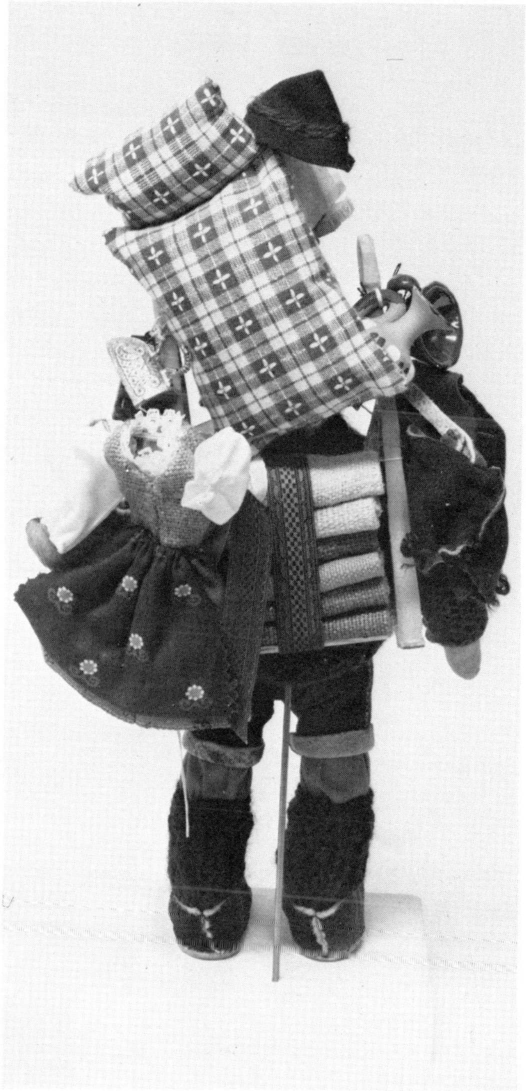

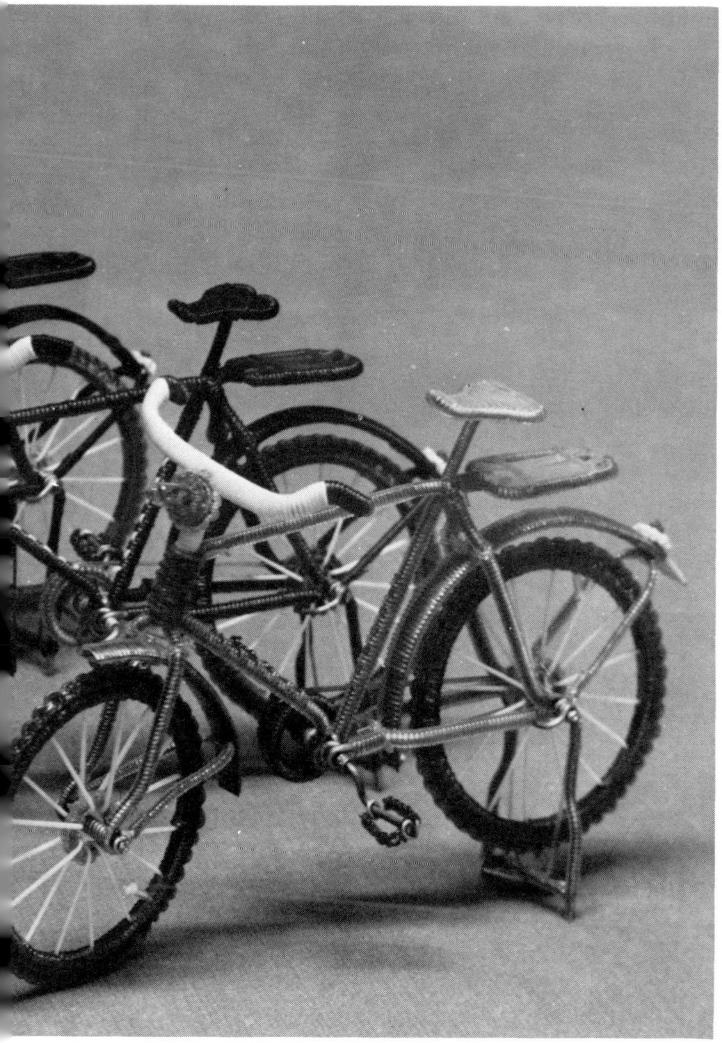

Tiny bicycles (left) were made from wire by craftsmen in the People's Republic of China. From the IFAF Collection (each bicycle 18.5 cm. long).

people of the state. This outstanding collection of eighteenth and nineteenth century folk art represents not only a major aspect of the cultural patrimony of Spanish New Mexicans but also serves to illuminate the role the Spanish played in settling the American West. Religious paintings on panels (*retablos*) and statuary (*bultos*) are complemented by a wide range of artistic and utilitarian objects made and used in New Mexico, such as furniture, household items, textiles, and tools.

The perceptive Historical Society of New Mexico was the first organization in the state to save colonial objects by acquiring items as early as the second half of the nineteenth century. It donated its collections to the Museum of New Mexico in 1977.

In the 1920s the Spanish Colonial Arts Society also began to collect fine examples of New Mexican folk art. Its outstanding holdings are on extended loan to the museum. In 1953, Cady Wells, one of the Spanish Colonial Arts Society's prominent members, donated the first major collection in this area to the museum. The Charles D. Carroll bequest in 1971 was another highly important acquisition of New Mexican works. The International Folk Art Foundation continues steadfastly to concentrate on collecting in this area.

Also in the care of the museum is the Spanish Colonial segment of the Fred Harvey Fine Arts Collection, which is not limited to New

Tiny crowns from Bolivia, Peru and Chile were originally made for religious statues. A bequest of Edith Page Skewes-Cox (tallest crown is 10.2 cm. high).

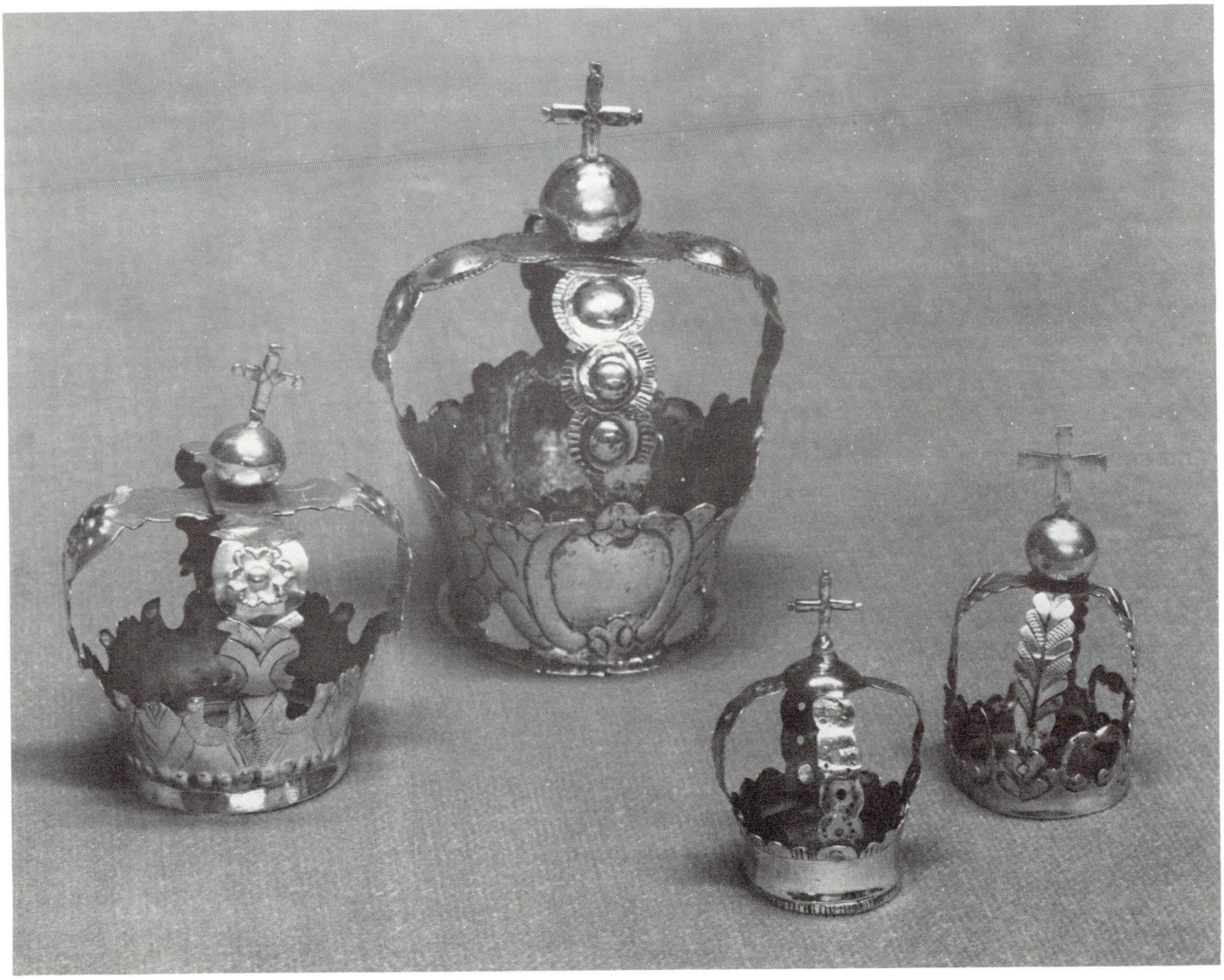

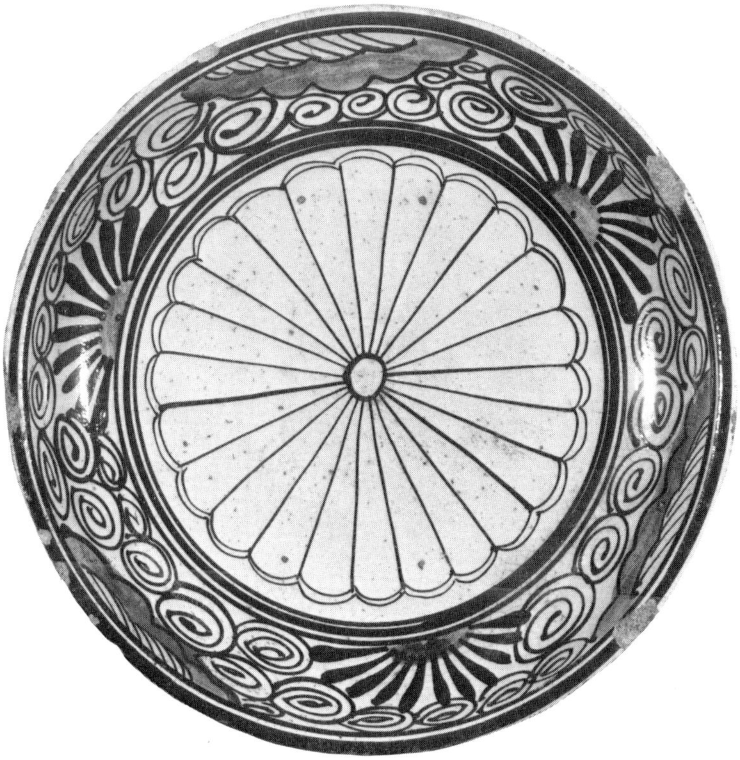

Decorated plate (right) originated in Seto, Japan. A gift of Hans A. Ries (26 cm. diameter).

Exquisite silver sidesaddle stirrup was made in Bolivia early in the nineteenth century. A bequest of Lucia Fox Edwards (22.5 cm. long).

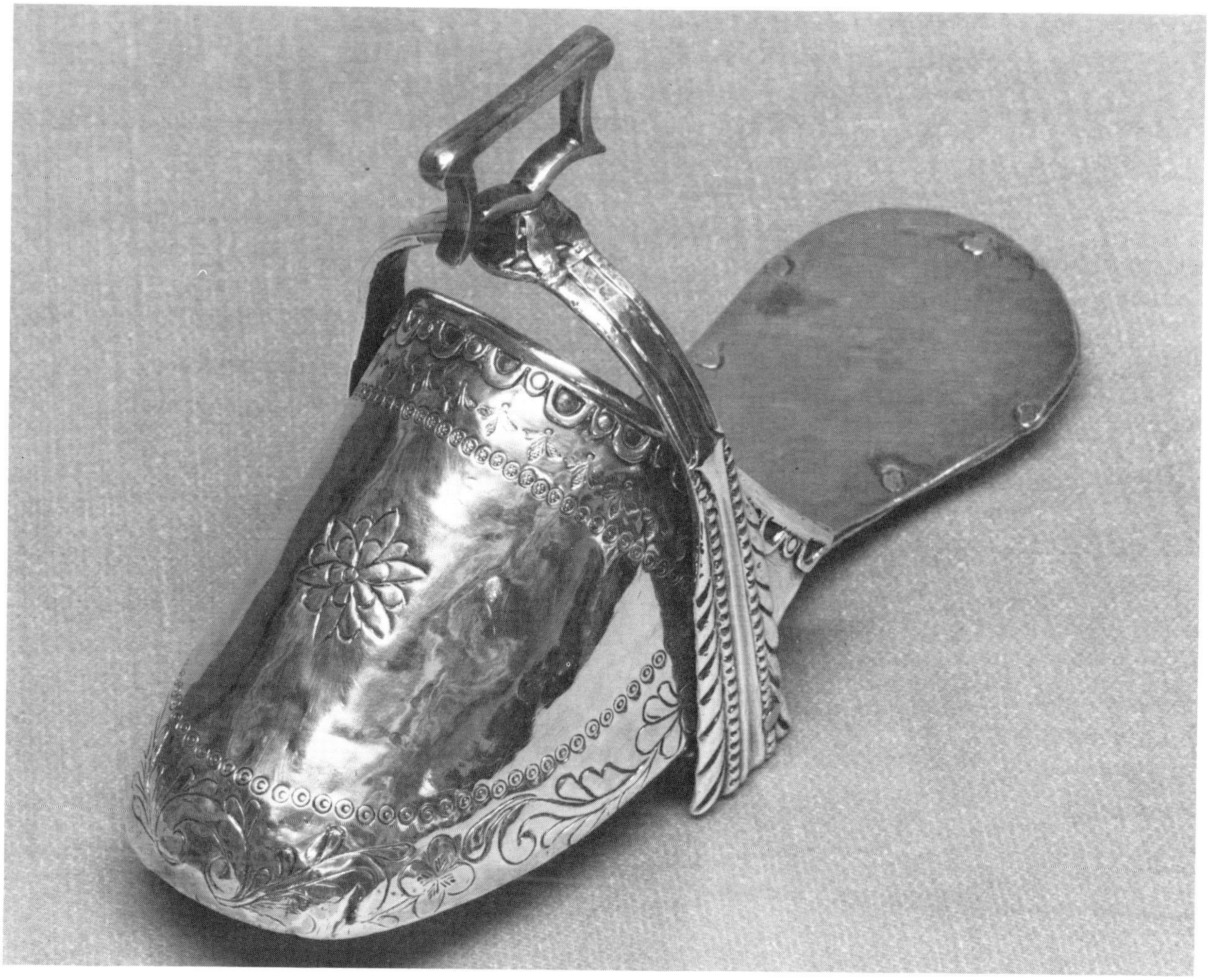

At the heart of any great museum are its curators. From top: Nora Fisher, Curator of Textiles; Charlene Cerny, Curator of American/Latin American Folk Art, with Judy Cohen, Curator of European Folk Art; Carol Steiro, Curator of Collections; Christine Mather, Curator of Spanish Colonial Art.

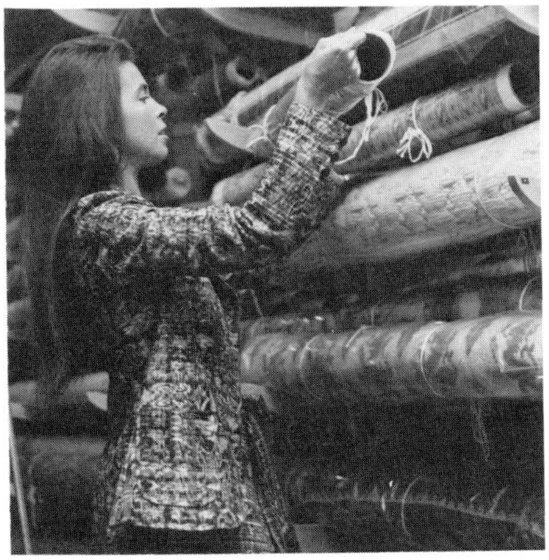

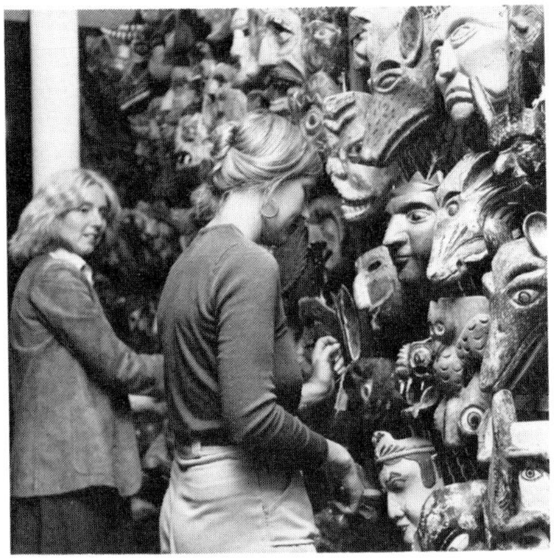

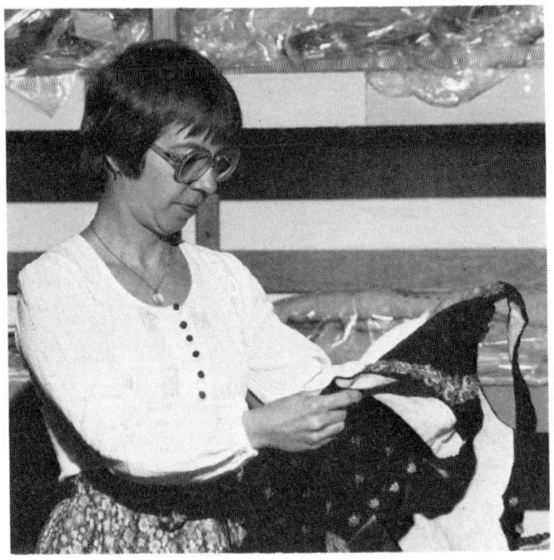

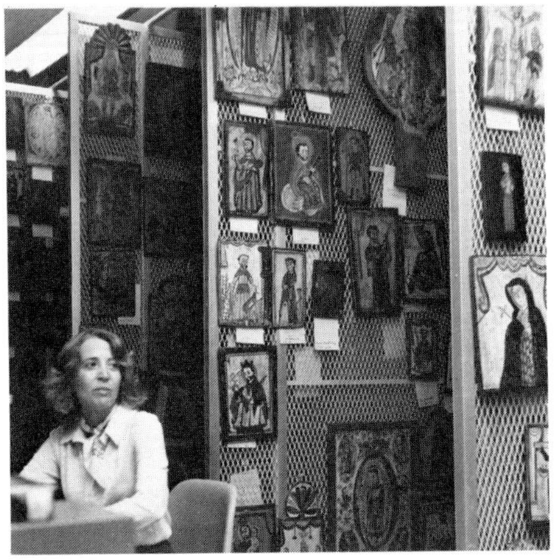

Mexican objects. This collection is in keeping with the museum's policy of emphasizing religious art from other countries formerly under Spanish hegemony. For that reason, countries such as Bolivia, Colombia, Ecuador, Guatemala, Mexico, Paraguay, Peru, the Philippines, Portuguese Goa, and the Commonwealth of Puerto Rico, are also represented.

As durable as it is beautiful is a group of Mexican *majolica* (lead and tin glazed ceramics) which survived the 1906 San Francisco earthquake, and was later given as the Houghton Sawyer Collection to the Museum of New Mexico. Recognizing the significance of the Mexican majolica, the International Folk Art Foundation directed authorities Florence and Robert Lister to purchase additional examples of Spanish and Mexican majolica for comparative study and display.

The Museum of International Folk Art leaves the collection of Native American art to other units of the Museum of New Mexico that specialize in this field. Exception is made for specimens considered departures from traditional Native American arts, such as Navajo pictorial weaving or Huichol yarn paintings. Two recent gifts from Sallie Wagner include a Tesuque Pueblo ceramic nativity and a "storyteller" clay figure made by Helen Cordero of Cochiti.

Folk art, until recently, was more casually appraised and sold than fine or academic art. Collectors had greater opportunity to indulge private passions, a fact demonstrated by the generic variety of folk art assemblages. Consider, for example, the Thorington Collection. In 1927 J. Monroe Thorington began to gather together objects of beauty and curiosity during his travels in the Austrian, French, Italian, and Swiss Alps. He later gave these items to MOIFA. The Philadelphia dentist, an avid mountain climber, had a good eye for the tools and household objects which now complement the museum's other collections of European domestic articles. Most impressive of the pieces in the Thorington gift is an assortment of painted and chip-carved wooden boxes and carved horn snuff boxes. Striking contrast to these specimens is offered by Janet Rosenwald's donation of unornamented, stamped and papered boxes of birchwood from Scandinavia, Western Europe, and the United States.

Not surprisingly, various collections of Mexican art are among the museum's best. Besides Mexican Indian costumes and jewelry, MOIFA owns a thoroughly representative group of figurative ceramics, including wedding and funeral scenes such as those made by Mexico's celebrated Teodora Blanco. The International Folk Art Foundation recently purchased 228 Mexican dance masks, and the museum's assortment of lacquerware has been enhanced by the recent gift of several valuable pieces from the René d'Harnoncourt Collection.

The museum staff hopes that someday its South American collections will be as well developed as its Mexican holdings. The museum is particularly proud of its figurative ceramics from Brazil. The pieces

Tinwork mirror (right), made in New Mexico late in the last century, is a gift of Florence Dibell Bartlett (68.5 cm.).

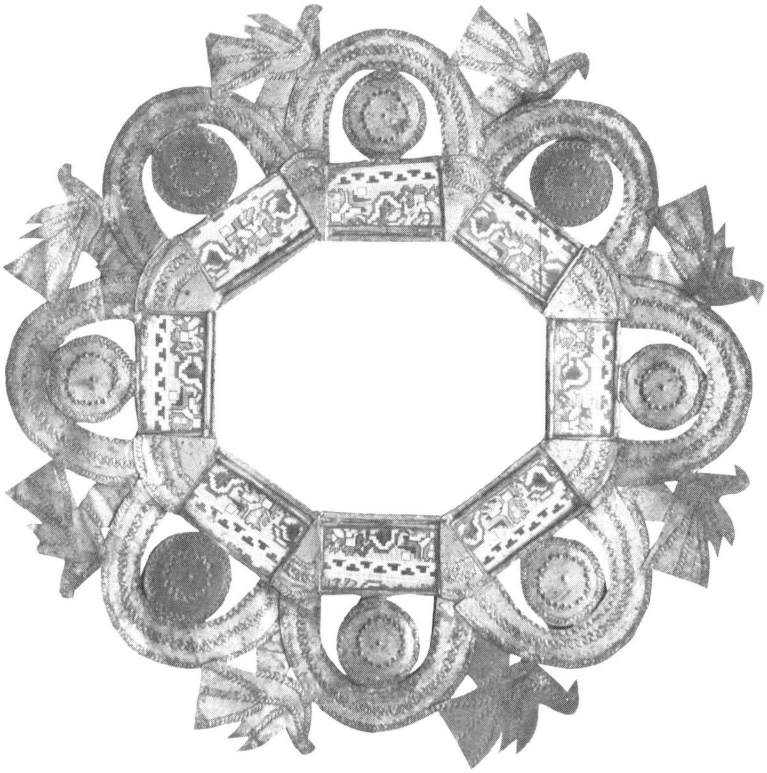

A glimpse of a section of the Latin American storage area at the Museum of International Folk Art (below).

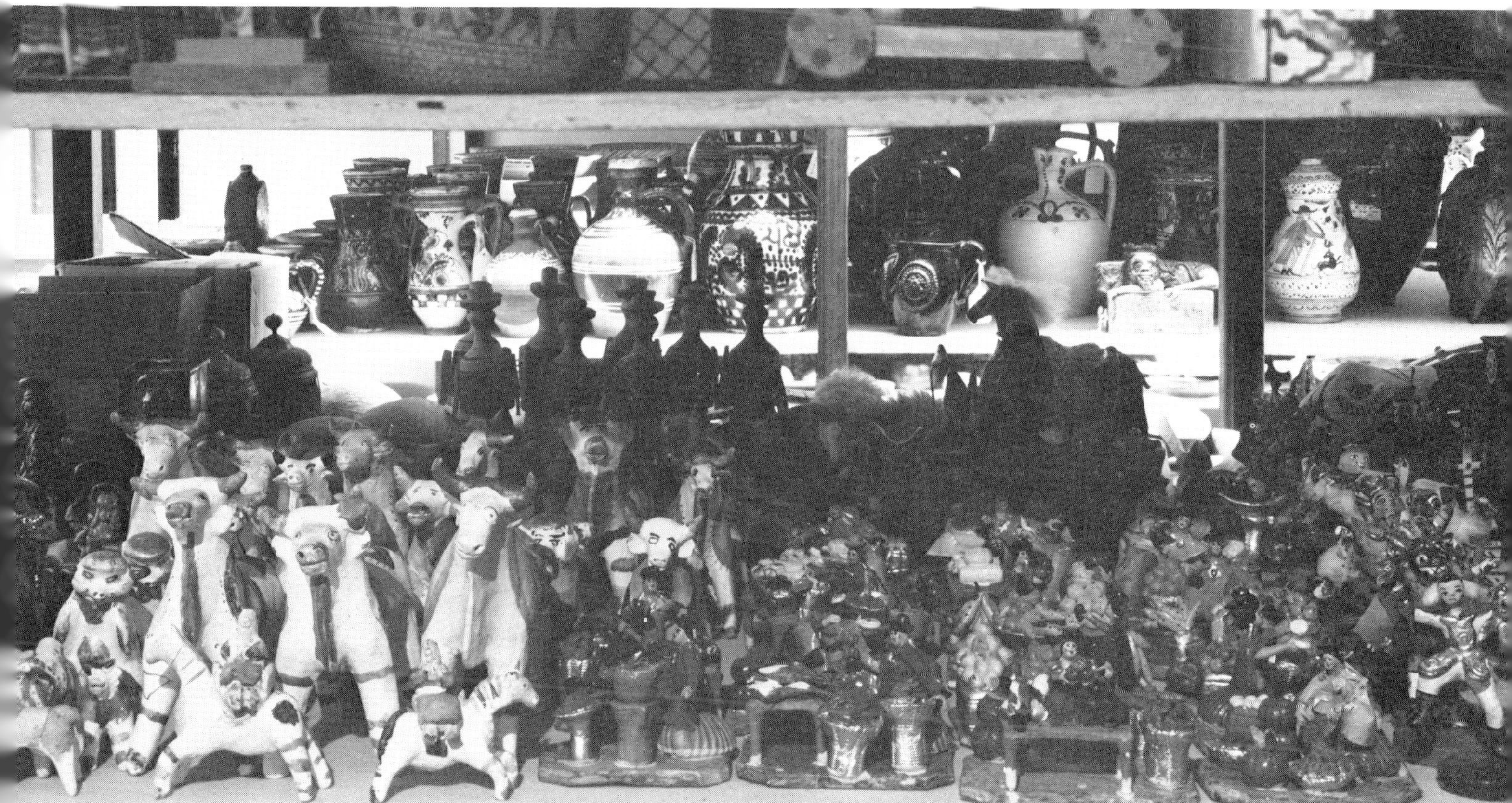

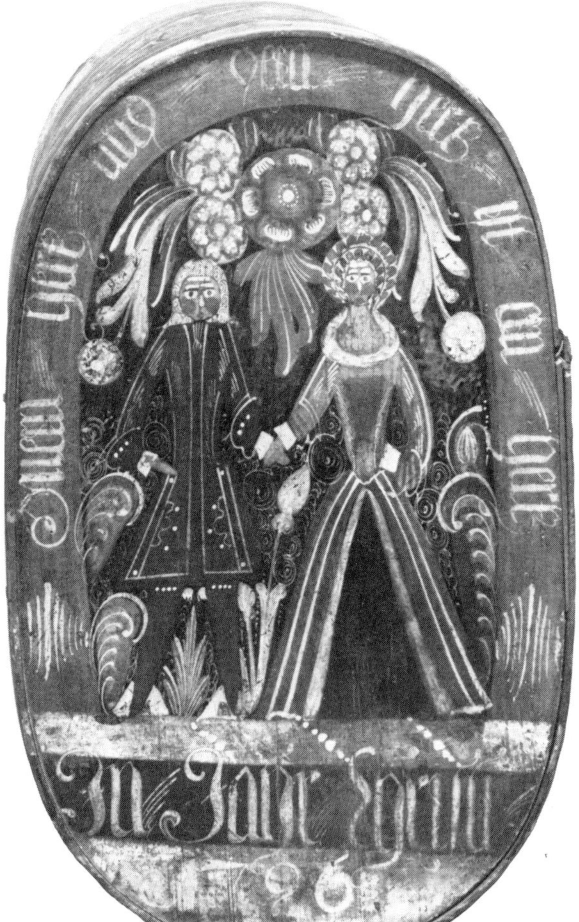

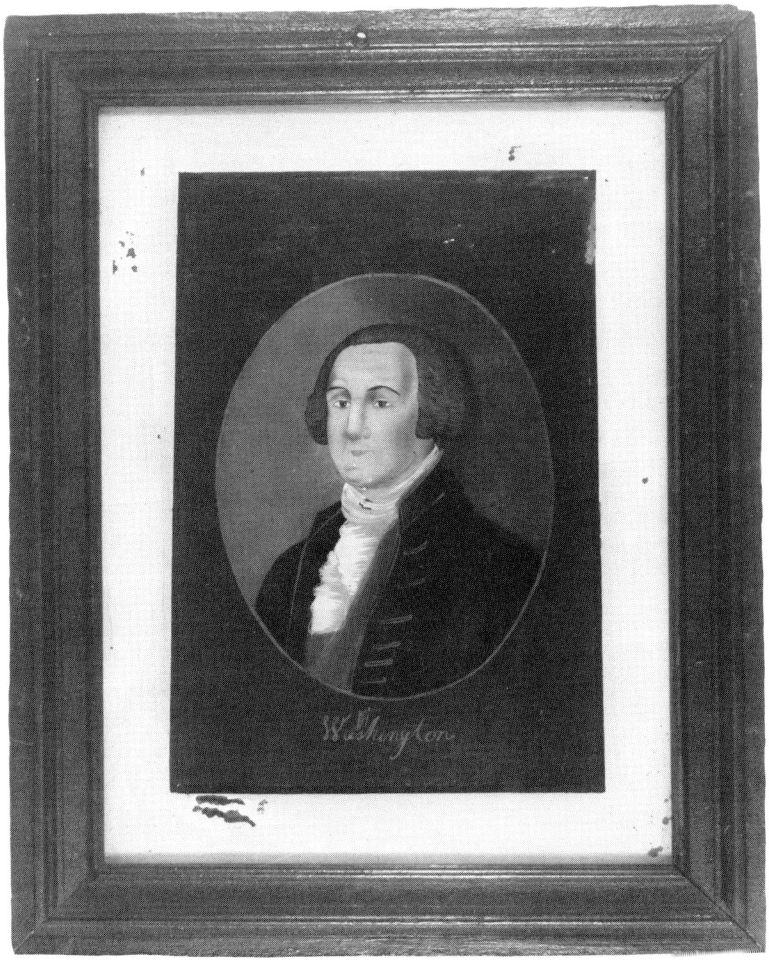

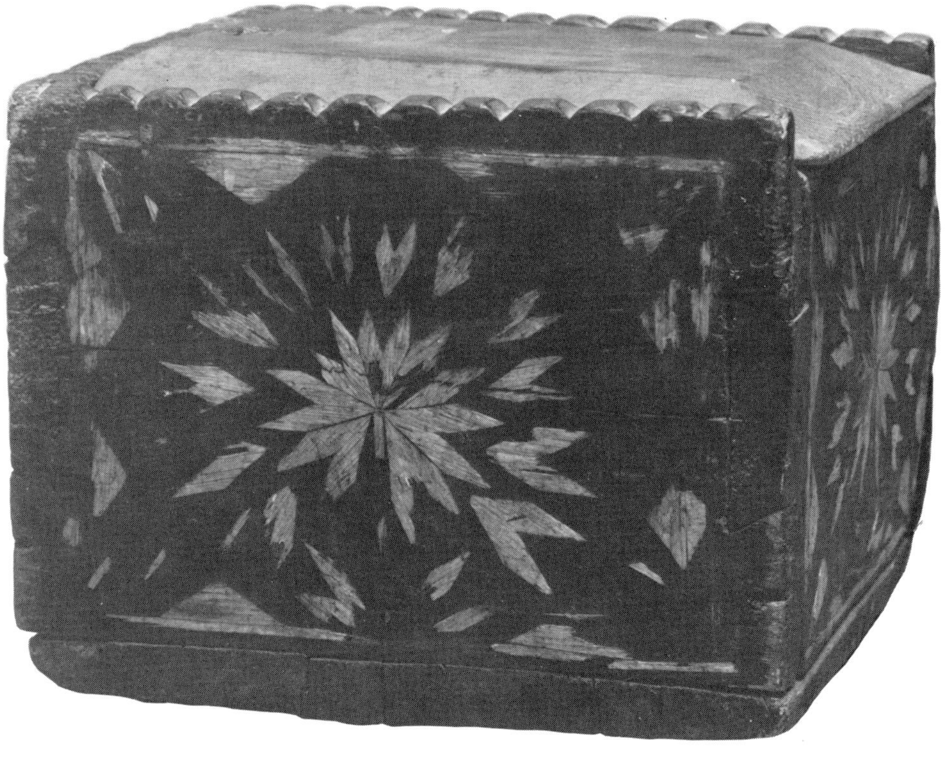

were collected by Katarina Real-Cate who lived for many years in that country. Her familiarity with the field is borne out by the distinct superiority of her purchases. Her gifts—as well as a group of figurative ceramics purchased for the International Folk Art Foundation by Jim Drum, director of exhibitions for the Museum of New Mexico—enrich the South American holdings and allow useful and interesting comparison with the Mexican figurative ceramics.

A small collection of Eastern American folk art items was recently enhanced by the addition of selected pieces from the Hemphill Collection. Herbert W. Hemphill, a founder and former curator of the Museum of American Folk Art in New York, has amassed a fine collection of American folk art dating from the nineteenth century to the present. The International Folk Art Foundation has thus far purchased thirteen weather vanes and whirligigs from Mr. Hemphill, who kindly donated a contemporary woodcarving and a weathervane from his collection to the museum. Each piece of this acquisition is distinguished by the originality, if not the idiosyncrasy, of its maker's vision.

Few casual visitors suspect that bequests are a means by which collections are enriched. Among the most recent of the museum's benefactors by bequest are the late Cyrus Baldridge, Dorothy Benrimo, Vivian Sloan Fiske, Anne Higham, and Mable Morrow.

The wide-ranging gift by the Girard Foundation will produce the most dramatic changes to date in the scope of the collections and exhibitions of the Museum of International Folk Art. This treasure, assembled by Mr. and Mrs. Alexander H. Girard, is a virtually inexhaustible wealth of folk art which spans the world, and at the same time unites it with a sense of common humanity with which every piece was collected. Toys dominate the collection, and it also includes nativities, figurative ceramics, fiber arts, and various miniatures. The collection is a playful assortment, coaxing good humor and giving full expression to fantasy.

The Girard Foundation Collection rounds out many of the museum's earlier holdings. The museum has maintained and improved upon accumulations of costumes, jewelry and domestic objects from Europe and Asia. It has built strong collections of Spanish Colonial and Latin American arts. As the quality and variety of all these collections have grown, so the Museum of International Folk Art has extended itself to a fairly encompassing representation of the world's folk art.

Opposite page: Bride's box from Germany (upper left) was given to MOIFA by Florence Dibell Bartlett (46.7 cm. long). "Washington," a reverse painting on glass, is a gift of Lucia Batten to the IFAF Collection (30 cm. high). New Mexican straw inlaid box (below), made in the mid-1800s, is a gift of the Historical Society of New Mexico (22.5 cm. wide).

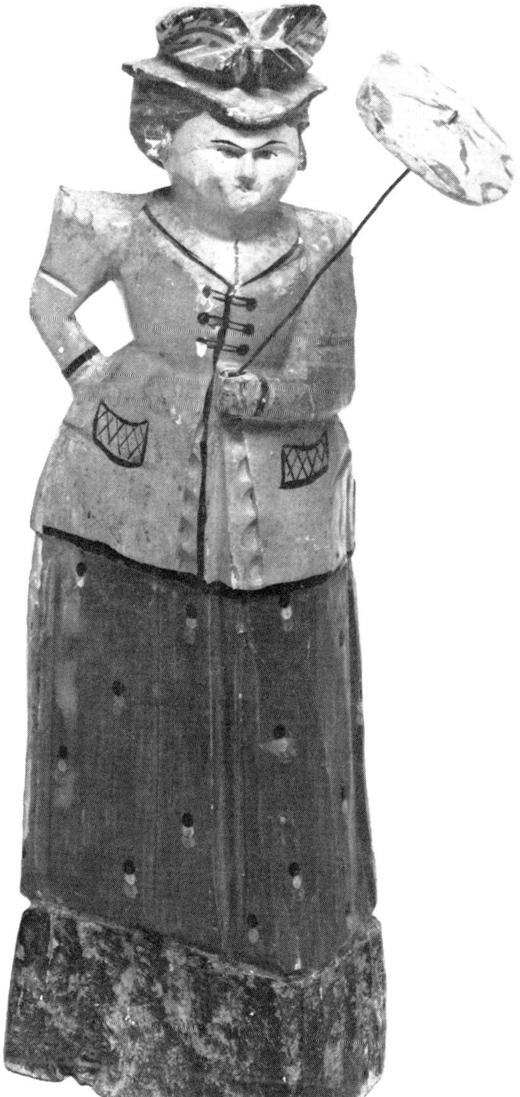

Right: Doll from Russia, made about 1910, was presented to the museum by Mrs. Edgar L. Rossin.

GIRARD FOUNDATION COLLECTION SPARKS EXPANSION PLANS

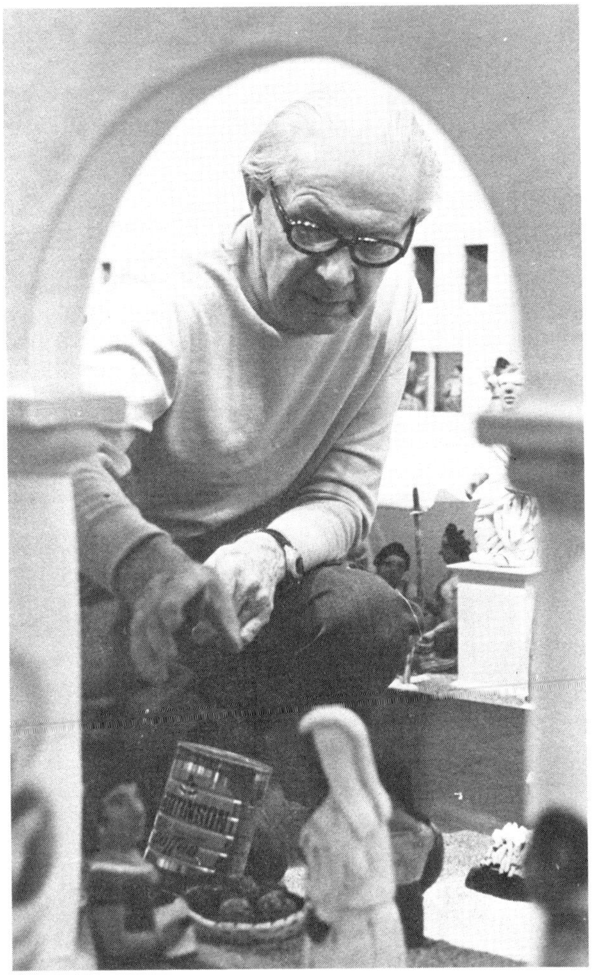

Alexander Girard, one of the world's foremost private collectors of folk art, installs Mexican village array in "Fantasy and Enchantment."

By Paul Winkler
Assistant Director,
Museum of International Folk Art

THE SILVER JUBILEE of the Museum of International Folk Art also heralds its greatest period of expansion. The recent gift of the Girard Foundation Collection is the single most important acquisition of the museum since its beginning. A lifelong endeavor of Mr. and Mrs. Alexander H. Girard, the collection contains sculptures, toys, paintings, textiles and other related objects originating from a wide number of countries and varying time spans.

The collection is not simply an amassment of objects but reflects the idea of Alexander Girard that such objects incorporate incalculable educational value. With his view that the collection "will communicate a few of the unsophisticated but inspired qualities of creative thought," the items were gathered for the purpose of illustrating and communicating the art, philosophy, and lifestyles of different peoples of the world, the underlying motives and bonds which exist among them, and the value of the objects in their relationship to contemporary life.

A perfect complement to the existing collections at the Museum of International Folk Art, the Girard Foundation gift increases the size of the museum's holdings *fivefold,* to over 120,000 items. Realizing the importance of such an acquisition and the physical expansion it demands, the Legislature of the State of New Mexico appropriated $1.5 million in February 1978 for the construction of a new wing at MOIFA where the collection will be housed.

The firm of Harvey Hoshour, Architect, Ltd. is in charge of designing the expansion project. Noted for sophistication and thoroughness in all aspects of its

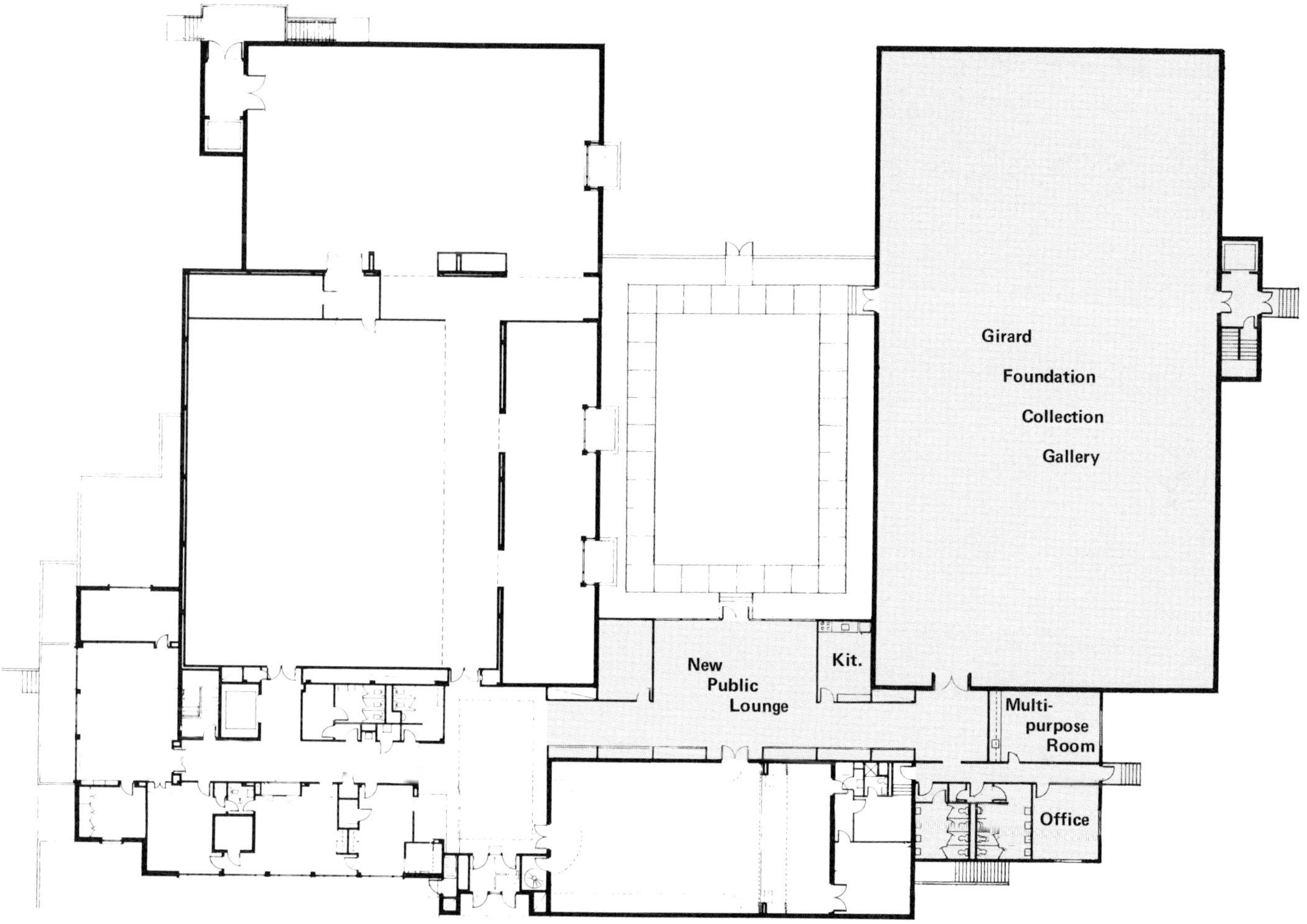

New Girard Foundation Wing will greatly increase exhibit area, as indicated on this floorplan of the main level, prepared by Harvey Hoshour, Architect, Ltd.

works, this architectural office has won numerous awards for design excellence. Recent projects have included the Indian Pueblo Cultural Center and the University of New Mexico Health Sciences Learning Resources Center, both in Albuquerque.

To a great extent, the design for the Girard Wing is based on the museum's approach to the presentation of objects. Exhibitions are developed according to a variety of concepts, and installations should be designed individually in order to project specific ideas the museum desires to convey. Where exhibitions are interpretative they demand a set traffic pattern of viewing for the sake of coherence; in contrast, those that stress visual delight ask for total freedom in the installation design. This kind of flexibility is best facilitated by an open shell building.

The Girard Wing will have 27,323 square feet of floor space. The exhibition area, encompassing 10,500 square feet, has been designed as a column-free, flexible space which will permit a maximum of varied approaches to installations. In keeping with modern trends, special electrical, lighting, temperature, humidity control, security and safety systems are being provided for throughout the wing. Non-display areas will be arranged for storage of that part of the collection not on show, a reception/lounge for the public, and offices.

The firm of Johnson, Hotvedt, DiNisco and Associates, Inc., Architects and Planners, Boston, was engaged in 1977 to compile a *Master Plan Report* for the museum, concurrent with the planning phase of the Girard Wing. Its purpose was to set guidelines for the

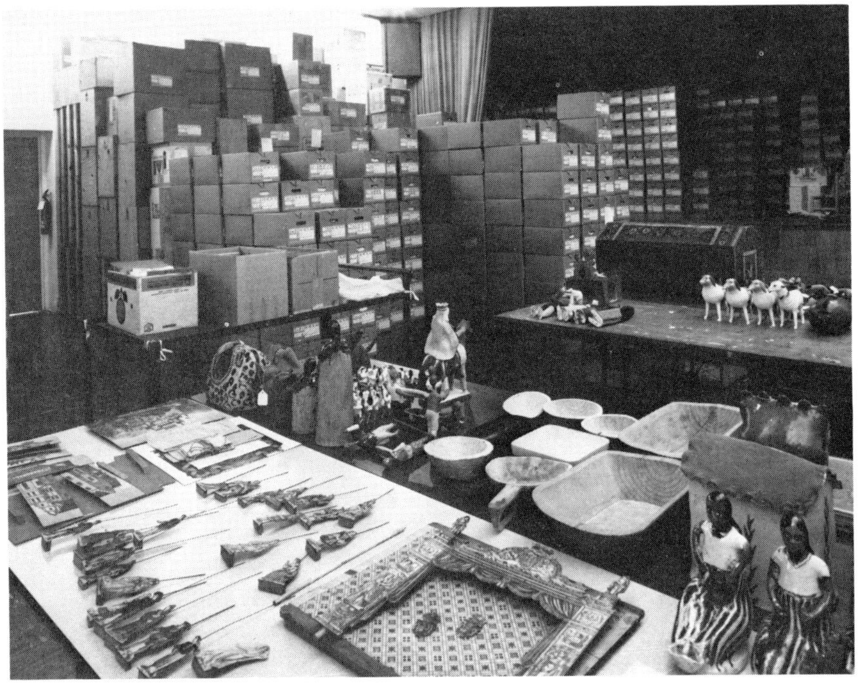

A part of the vast Girard Foundation Collection being prepared for cataloguing in MOIFA's auditorium.

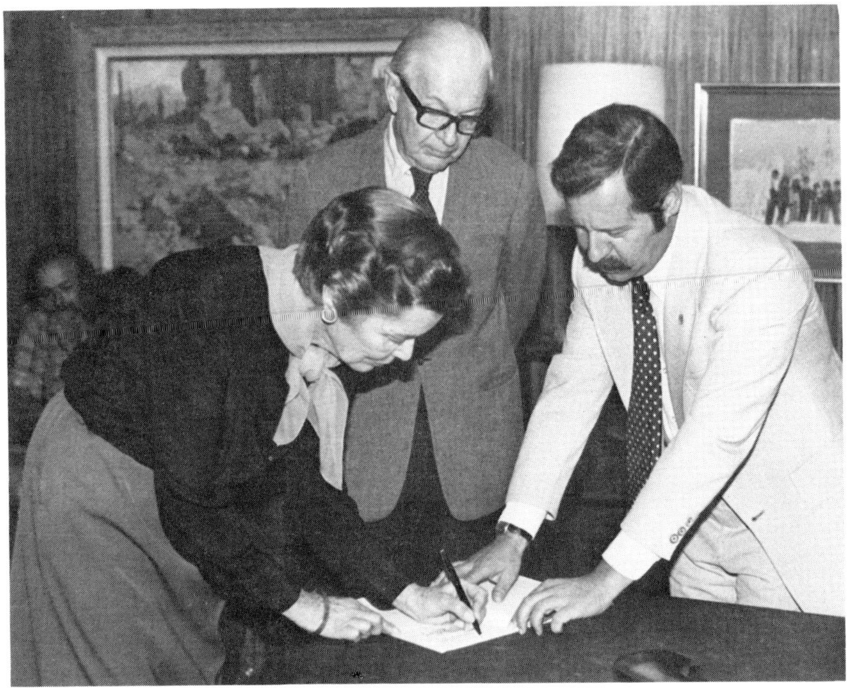

Mrs. Susan Girard, Alexander Girard, and Harry Wugalter, Secretary of the Department of Educational Finance and Cultural Affairs, sign agreement gifting Collection to the state on October 19, 1978.

renovation of the existing MOIFA building and guidelines for potential new facilities whose establishment is made all the more imperative by the construction of the Girard Wing. Such new facilities are to include curatorial office and collections research areas, exhibition preparation and workshop areas, and a permanent gallery for the display of the important Spanish Colonial Art collection. Harvey Hoshour has produced schematic drawings for these projected additions. The comprehensive master plan was made possible through the generous support of the International Folk Art Foundation, the Museum of New Mexico Foundation, and the National Endowment for the Arts.

The museum now has a logical and sound plan for long-range development. Phased implementation is now a matter of meeting the financial requirements. It is the earnest hope of the Museum of New Mexico that strong support from several quarters will be forthcoming, as the Museum of International Folk Art has an unexcelled potential for ranking as one of the great folk art museums of the world. The $1.5 million appropriation by New Mexico's state legislators is a mark of confidence in such a future and sets the museum firmly on the road to excellence.

AMERICAN FOLK ART COLLECTION BRINGS IT ALL HOME

The Museum of International Folk Art is fortunate to house a number of outstanding collections: costumes and textiles from around the world, Mexican folk art, Spanish Colonial silver, majolica and religious art, including that of New Mexico. But American folk art has not been an area which received much attention in the past. The collections, until recently, reflected that fact . . .

By Charlene Cerny
Curator of American and
Latin American Folk Art

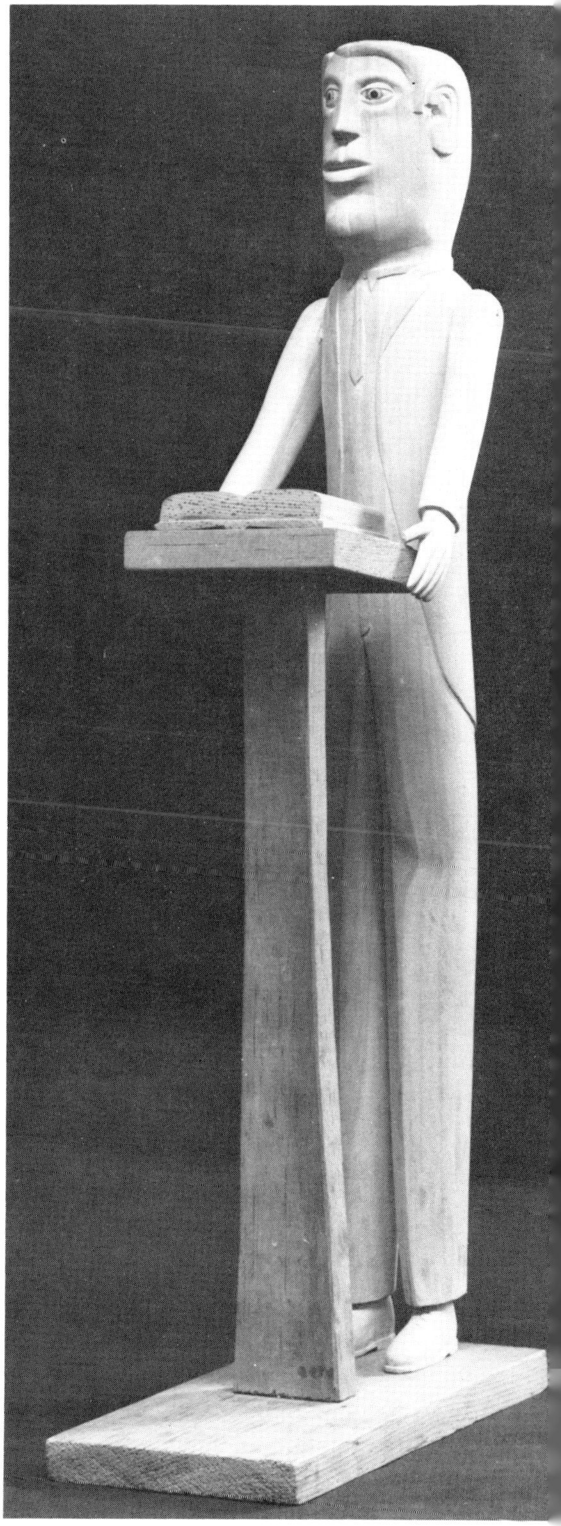

Tall preacher was carved by Edgar Tolson of Campton, Kentucky in 1971 (70 cm. high).

WE LOOKED rather woefully over the goods: a few quilts, some nice coverlets, a handful of tools and animal gear, maybe a couple dozen good stoneware pots. Not a weathervane, a whirligig, or a cigar store Indian in the lot. Certainly not a selection representative of America's incredibly vital folk tradition. The question presented itself: how would the Museum of International Folk Art ever achieve the "truly international character" its foundress Florence Dibell Bartlett had envisioned, when it had so little of America's folk art to share with others?

The answer has come, in part, through a concerted effort by the museum and the International Folk Art Foundation in partnership with the federal government—an effort which would not only have pleased Miss Bartlett were she alive today, but no doubt would have amazed her as well. For in the 1950s, when the museum was only a fledgling institution, opportunities for aid to museums were virtually non-existent, except for gifts from private patrons. It was not until 1965 that Congress created the National Endowment for the Arts, an executive level agency charged with administering funds appropriated to support arts activities. Then, in 1968, the Museum Purchase Plan was initiated.

The Museum Purchase Plan is a program whereby matching grants are made available to qualifying institutions for the purchase of works by living American artists. The stated objectives of the program are to "encourage museums to add to their collections of contemporary

American art, to create and expand public response to works by living artists through display of their works, to raise new funds for this purpose specifically, and to provide direct financial assistance for artists." In other words, it is one of those rare situations in which everyone involved stands to gain and nobody loses.

So it was in 1974 that MOIFA first approached the National Endowment for support to increase its collection of contemporary American folk art. A grant in the amount of $5,000 was sought and subsequently awarded. This amount was generously matched dollar-for-dollar by the International Folk Art Foundation, thus enabling the museum to acquire some forty new pieces of American folk art in the years 1975 and 1976. Existing collections of Southwestern folk art had not kept abreast of current trends, so it was decided early on that the focus of this initial grant would be the work of contemporary New Mexican artisans. Several staff trips to the homes and workshops of often isolated craftsmen proved fruitful. Commissions were arranged with the more established artists while arts and crafts fairs and word-of-mouth suggestions uncovered some previously unrecognized talents.

Because the woodcarving tradition in New Mexico had, since the prolific nineteenth century *santeros,* been a strong one, several contemporary woodcarvings ranging from the distinctly traditional to the wildly innovative were acquired. Joining existing collections were, among other things, unpainted Cordova-style carvings by Frances Romero and Gloria Lopez Cordova. Three woodcarvings by Luis Tapia of Santa Fe reflect this young craftsman's fresh viewpoint; his depiction of the Nativity, for example, suggests the presence of an angel overhead by wings and face alone, a bravura shorthand. Another of the more substantial acquisitions in woodcarving is a life-size

Nativity by woodcarver Luis Tapia of Santa Fe (49.4 cm. high).

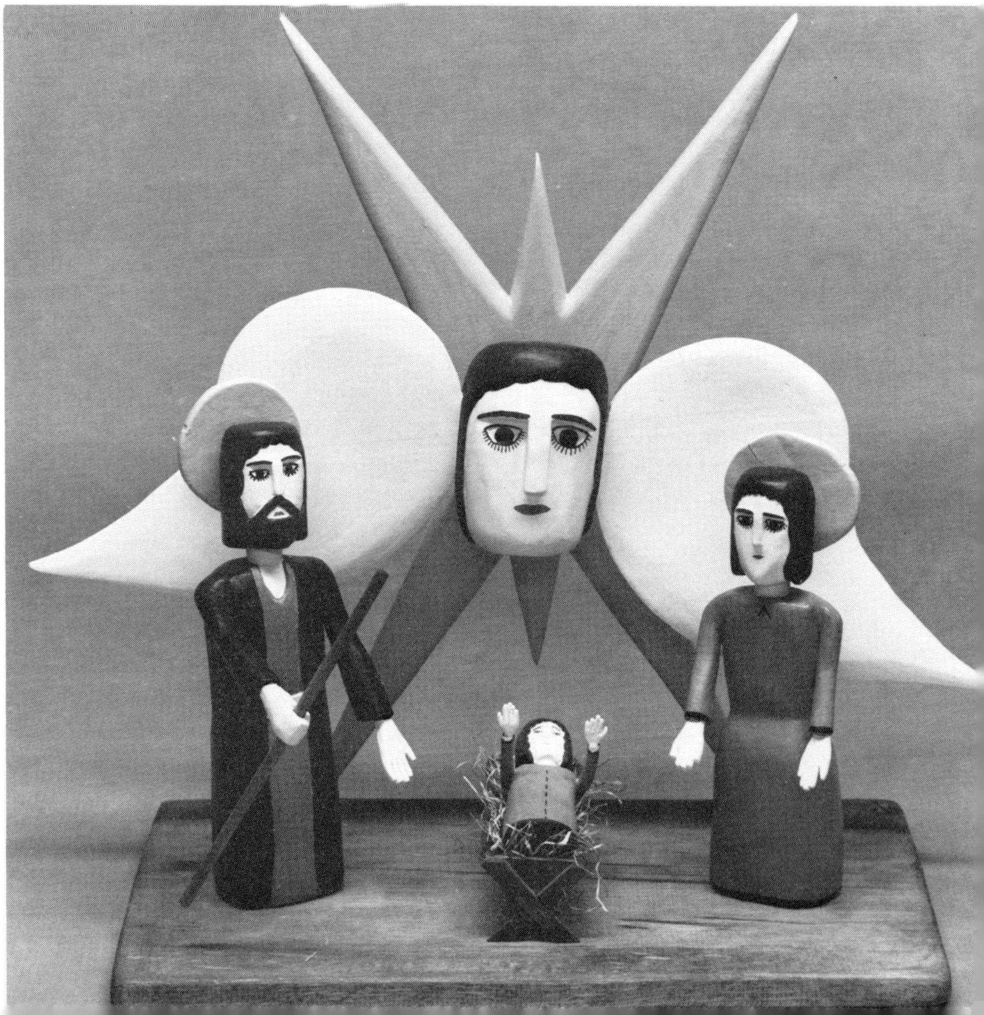

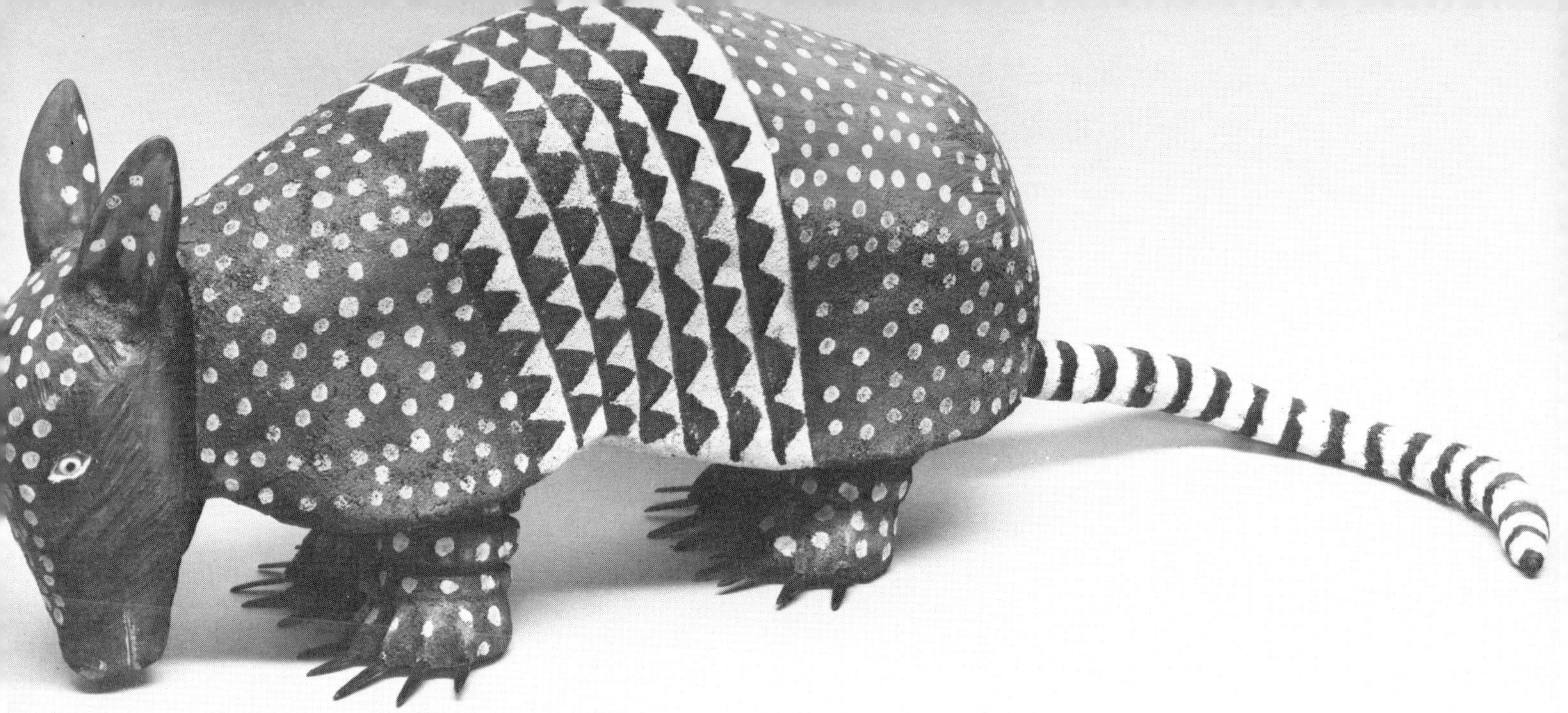

Armadillo cleverly carved by Felipe B. Archuleta of Tesuque, New Mexico (38.5 cm. long).

painted armadillo by well-known folk sculptor Felipe B. Archuleta of Tesuque. Its horny shell pattern was imaginatively recreated with spots applied by a cigarette filter dipped in paint.

Woven textiles by John R. Trujillo of Chimayó and David Salazar of Ribera, New Mexico, evidence the fact that the Rio Grande textile tradition lives on, though few craftsmen still weave the old patterns. Also acquired locally was a delicately ornamented clay figure by famed Cochiti potter Helen Cordero, who originated the popular "storyteller." A "storyteller" figure by Alma Concha of Taos Pueblo aptly demonstrates how contemporary designs spread with ease from one pueblo to another.

More in the mainstream of American folk art were two works acquired from the late Santa Fe painter Camille Blair. *Miners, Virginia City* is considered to be one of her finest works. Other notable purchases were a large and colorful Mardi Gras scene by retired fireman "Chief" P. L. Wiley of Louisiana, and an elaborate painted and glittered wood-carved panel by Elijah Pierce of Ohio, one of a series of religious works which once lined the walls of his Columbus barbershop.

Citing the "surprisingly little energy being expended by public institutions in the acquisition of such works," MOIFA director Yvonne Lange in December 1976 again approached the National Endowment for support. The initial grant had enabled the museum to update its collections of New Mexican folk art as well as to begin a modest collection of objects from other parts of the United States. This grant—for a requested $10,000 with an equal match—was to spark an even more intense effort to develop the non-Southwestern portion of the American folk art collection.

In July 1977, U.S. Senator Pete V. Domenici of New Mexico announced that the second grant, in the amount requested, had been approved. This money was subsequently matched by another $10,000 grant awarded by the trustees of the International Folk Art Foundation. And the search for appropriate objects was on again!

While only half the funds from this grant have been expended at the time of this writing, the growing collection of contemporary American folk art is already one unparalleled in any other U.S. museum. With the possible exception of Williamsburg's Abby Aldrich Rockefel-

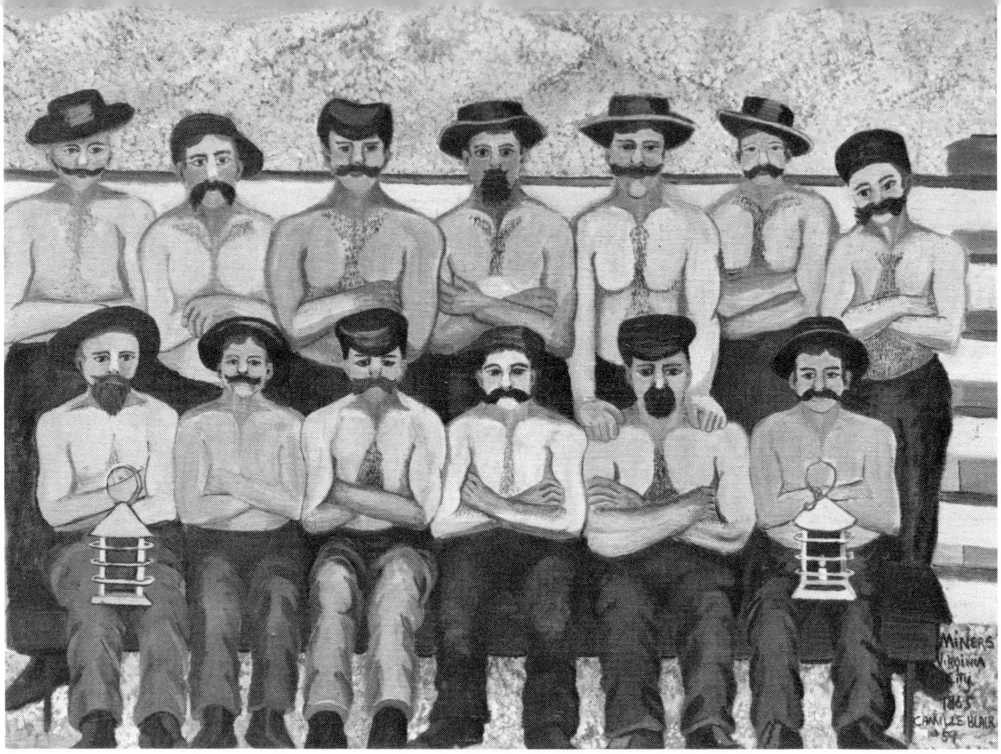

"Miners, Virginia City," painting in primitive technique by Camille Blair of Santa Fe, 1959 (46 cm. wide).

ler Folk Art Collection and the Museum of American Folk Art in New York, few institutions have been giving priority to developing collections in this area. It is a disturbing fact that the far greater number of major pieces are entering private collections at a fast pace.

Sculpture in wood has always been a favorite medium of expression for the American folk artists, and today is no exception. A powerful woodcarving by Edgar Tolson of Campton, Kentucky exemplifies this craft at its finest. The preacher's stiff posture and tight-lipped countenance make for an unforgettable authoritarian image. Quite the opposite in feeling are Miles Carpenter's *Sow and Seven Piglets* made in Waverly, Virginia in 1973, an affectionate look at one of nature's more unappreciated species.

Five paintings have been purchased thus far from the grant monies, the most notable of which is a major work by Harry Lieberman of Great Neck, New York. Entitled *The Mystique of Life*, this 30-by-40-inch canvas summarizes the centenarian artist's philosophy of life, illustrating through six vignettes man's struggle to overcome his difficulties.

A large portrait of George Washington dominates the composition of Reverend Howard Finster's *Our First and Last Leaders of the Truth*. This painting eulogizes those whom preacher and repairman Finster considers to be the world's foremost truth tellers: Jesus Christ, George Washington, Bobby Kennedy, and himself. Certainly less presumptuous and rather more typical of the "sweet-style" of American naive painting is Barbara Strawser's *Christmas*. This winter scene includes carolers, a Nativity, and a Santa on skis for a holiday potpourri which merges the secular and the religious, the old and the new.

Coincident with the museum's effort, the International Folk Art Foundation has also greatly expanded its purchases in American folk art. Additional holdings belonging to the Foundation and housed in the museum add immeasurably to both the breadth and scope of the collection. A mint condition pictorial hooked rug from Pennsylvania, and what has been termed by a visiting quilt specialist as the "finest example yet" of a *broderie perse* quilt, were both recently acquired. Another important addition was a beautiful painted Pennsylvania Ger-

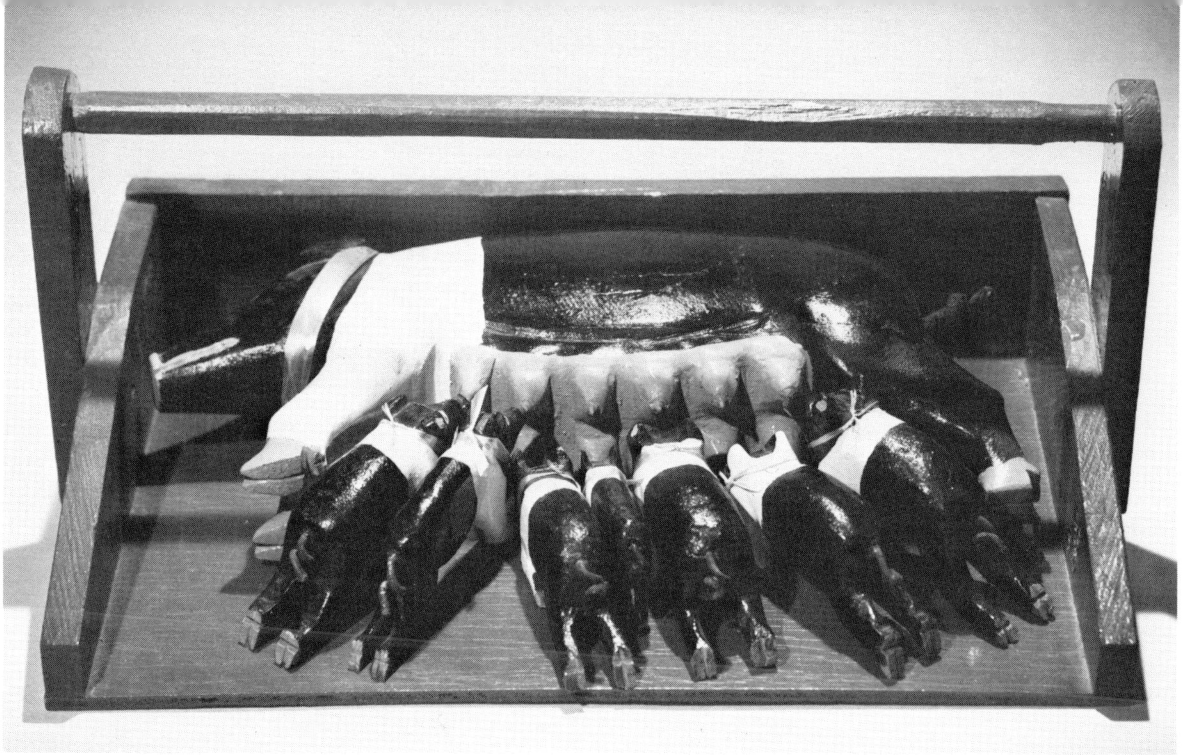

man dower chest. But perhaps the most significant acquisition to date has been the purchase of thirteen whirligigs and weather vanes from the Herbert W. Hemphill, Jr. Collection. This group of wind toys and indicators contains unique examples of these forms dating from the early nineteenth century to about 1930. Outstanding are a whimsical Hessian soldier whirligig whose arms flail unceremoniously in the breeze, and a fish weather vane found in Maine whose pieced mica surface is an ingenious substitute for scales.

"Sow and Seven Piglets" carved by Miles Carpenter of Waverly, Virginia in 1973 (46.3 cm. long).

In addition, the generosity of private collectors has aided substantially in the development of an American folk art collection at the museum. Making significant additions to the textile holdings have been Mrs. Evan Randolph and Gertrude Clarke, who donated very fine quilts, and Mrs. Lucia Batten who gifted a number of embroidered samplers among other things. William S. Huey contributed the first hand carved decoys to the collection, which was later broadened by the addition of seven curlew decoys given by H. C. Randolph, Sr., and duck decoys from Sallie Wagner and H. Ross Smith. Jeffrey Camp and Van Deren Coke have given numerous pieces of American folk pottery. Herbert W. Hemphill, Jr. has contributed a well-documented stallion weathervane and an extraordinary woodcarving by Edgar Tolson which translates into wood the *Unicorn in the Garden,* the subject of the famed medieval tapestry at the Cloisters in New York. These, among other numerous gifts, have been much appreciated.

As seems always to be the case in the world of museums, though, we can see the need for even further help. Folk portraits and paintings of all kinds, shop signs and figures, decoys, quilts, and folk sculpture in general are all areas in need of further collections development. But with continued support provided by grants from the government and private organizations, and the interest of individual donors, the future development of our American folk art collection now seems assured. ▪

Four Horsemen whirligig from Ohio (ca. 1900) was purchased from the Herbert W. Hemphill, Jr. Collection by IFAF.

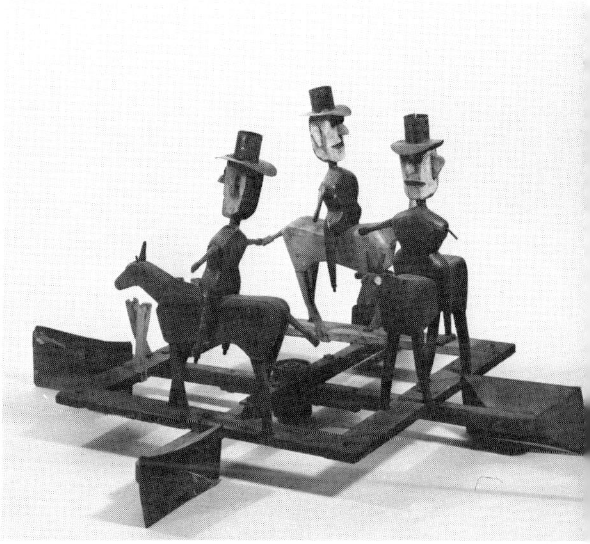

Acknowledgement

I wish to thank Julia Weissman for providing an edited transcript of Harry Lieberman's explanations of *The Mystique of Life* (in color, page 36), which she obtained from numerous interviews with the artist. Except for the whirligig, all pieces shown in this section (pp. 49-53) were purchased with the aid of funds from the National Endowment for the Arts and the International Folk Art Foundation.

Museum of International Folk Art Exhibitions, 1953-1978

OPENED 1953

The Bartlett Collection

OPENED 1954

Baffinland Eskimo Art
When Cultures Meet (Alaska and Mexico)
Beyond the Mask (Indian and Eskimo)
Lion-Dog in Chinese Popular Art
Swedish Christmas

OPENED 1955

Early American Folk Sculpture
Design Show
Warren Gilbertson Collection of Oriental Pottery
Craftsmen of New Mexico, 1955
Contemporary Wood Carving (Alaska)
Beauty in the World (Sweden)
Folk Art of Japan
Chinese Jade: The Witter Bynner Collection

OPENED 1956

Hungarian Folk Art
Fun and Fantasy
American Craftsmen
Decorative Arts of India
Children's Paintings from Japan and Sweden
Craftsmen of New Mexico, 1956
Polish Paper Cutouts
Potters' Exhibition
San Blas Appliqué
Argentine Children's Paintings
Folk Pottery
Scrimshaw

OPENED 1957

Color Is South (Mexico)
The Passion Play at Ixtapalapa (photographs)
The Word Is Shibui (Japan)
Craftsmen of New Mexico, 1957
One Europe

OPENED 1958

Jamini Roy (Indian folk artist)
Photographs of Sarawak
Indonesian Art
Craftsmen of New Mexico, 1958
The Moslem World

OPENED 1959

Guatemalan Textiles
Craftsmen of New Mexico, 1959
Popular Arts of Colonial New Mexico
Russian Icons
Selections from the Bartlett Collection

OPENED 1960

Melanesian Art
Norwegian Tapestries
Swedish Handicrafts
Tibetan Art
Craftsmen of New Mexico, 1960
Traditional New Mexico Crafts
Forms from Israel
Exhibit of Museum Publications
Seven Metals of Africa
Flag Display
El Santo Niño de Navidad

OPENED 1961

Many Lands
Objects from the Permanent Collection
Popular Arts of Yucatan
Greek Costumes and Embroidery
Nacimientos from the Alexander Girard Collection

OPENED 1962

Thai Paintings
Indigo
Folk Art of Lapland
Craftsmen of New Mexico, 1962
Recent Acquisitions: Installment I
Recent Acquisitions: Installment II
Rio Grande Blankets
Comparative Santos
Containers
Christmas World
Watercolor Renderings of Folk Toys

OPENED 1963

American Folk Art
Eskimo Prints (Baffin Island)
Photos of Contemporary Japanese Artists at Work
Rebecca James Colcha Needlework and Glass Paintings
Bonader (Swedish wall hangings) from the Bartlett Collection
The Idea of Folk Art
Scherenschnitten (scissors-cuts) by Walter von Gunten
Spanish Colonial Silver: IBM Acquisition
Intercultural Exhibition
Eighteenth Century Santeros of New Mexico
Huey Bird Decoy Collection
Pennsylvania German Folk Art
Craftsmen of New Mexico, 1963

OPENED 1964

One-Man Craft Shows
Jade Toggles and Buckles
Chinese Peasant Cottons
New Mexico Santos 1800-1850
Swedish Folk Art
Southwestern Craftsmen: Mary Elizabeth McDonald, David Ortega and Neal Townsend
1964 Indian Artists Annual Exhibition (Student Division)
Southwestern Craftsmen: Frank Long, Gisella Loeffler and Kelly Shannon
Southwestern Craftsmen: Rachel Brown, Charles Loloma, and Ralph Pardington
Five Continents: Gifts and Purchases

OPENED 1965

Patrocino Barela: Taos Woodcarver
Textiles from Java, Bali, and Sumatra;
  Shadow Figures from Siam (Extensions of Five
  Continents show)
Collage in Stitchery
Jewish Ceremonial Art
1965 Southwestern Craftsmen's Exhibition
Gyotaku (Japanese Fish-Prints)
The Shape of Music
Hearts and Flowers (Greeting Cards)

OPENED 1966

Afro-Arabic
Salt Glaze Technique
German Stoneware
1966 New Mexico Craftmen's Exhibition
Los Luceros Collection of Spanish Colonial Art

OPENED 1967

Equestrian Gear
Fabric for Living
1967 Southwest Craftsmen's Exhibition
Recent Acquisitions

OPENED 1968

Folk Art in Wood
Spanish Colonial Art
1968 New Mexico Craftsmen's Exhibition
Mini-Themes (small exhibitions shown four at a time)

OPENED 1969

1969 Southwest Craftsmen's Exhibition
The New Mexico Santero
Gravestone Rubbings from New England Cemeteries

OPENED 1970

Santa Fe Opera Poster Design Competition Entries
1970 New Mexico Craftsmen's Exhibition
World of Folk Costume
Open Storage Wing officially opened

OPENED 1971

1971 Southwestern Crafts Biennial
Frank Patania Jewelry Retrospective

OPENED 1972

1500 Years of Andean Weaving
1972 New Mexico Crafts Biennial
Embroideries from Ninhue, Chile
Recent Acquisitions
Southwestern Indian Nativities

OPENED 1973

Sculpture in Bread by Barbara Brody
Contemporary Roadside Folk Art (from the collection
  of Nina Howell Starr)
What Is Folk Art?
Quilts
The Wall Hangings of Irene Valdez
Aline Porter's Doll House
Birds and Polish Paper Cutouts
Traveling Limners
Easter Eggs
Jack Lenor Larsen Traveling Study Unit (textiles)
Goa Santos
Fiesta Crown
New Mexico Wood Carvers
Mexico: Fantasy and Imagination
Dolls

OPENED 1974

Recent Acquistions: Palestinian Costumes
Recent Acquisitions: Alpine Folk Art
  collected by James M. Thorington
Paintings by E. Boyd
Cobalt Glazed Ceramics
Japanese Paper Dolls
1974 New Mexico Crafts Biennial
African Fabrics
Lightsome: Windows and Lampshades by Jim
  and Charlotte Hollis
Village Embroidery Workshops
A Nacimiento by Teodora Blanco of Atzompa, Oaxaca,
  from the Girard Foundation Collection

OPENED 1975

1975 Southwest Crafts Biennial
Eveli: One-Man Exhibition
Maxmiliano Chavez: One-Man Exhibition
Navajo Pictorial Weaving
E. Boyd Memorial Exhibition
Behold, A Child Is Born (Nacimientos)

OPENED 1976

1976 New Mexico Crafts Biennial
Selections from the James Monroe Thorington Collection
Bolivian Market
Días de Más, Días de Menos; Days of Plenty, Days of Want:
  Spanish Folklife and Art in New Mexico
Araucanian Adornment
American Coverlets
Nacimientos

OPENED 1977

1977 Southwest Crafts Biennial
More Splendid than the Shining Full Moon:
  Costumes from Old Palestine
Santos y Milagros de Mexico from the
  Girard Foundation Collection
Isla Negra Embroideries
Fantasy and Enchantment: Selections from the
  Girard Foundation Collection
  (included Amulet, Talisman, Ex-voto exhibition)

OPENED 1978

Vision USA: Folk Art from the Collection of
  Herbert W. Hemphill, Jr.
Spanish Textile Tradition of New Mexico and Colorado
From Baroque to Folk: Spanish Colonial Art
  from the Permanent Collection

TRAVELING EXHIBITIONS, 1957-1971

Introduction to Folk Art
Costumes from Around the World
Man the Hunter (Arctic and Tropical)
Indian Art of the Americas
Tools and Woodworking of Spanish New Mexico
Climate of Man's Living
Desert People
The Idea of Folk Art
The Reindeer Followers
Magic and Medicine in Folk Art
People at the Top of the World
Mountain Folk of the Southern Appalachians
The Old in the New: Tracing the Folk Heritage
  of New Mexico
Adornment: the Image-Maker
Durable Metal: Timeless Art
Sculpture in the Southwest
Hats, Helmets and Crowns
Horses and Horsemen in the Southwest

Accolades for the Folk Art Museum

Dear Dr. Lange:

Please accept my warmest congratulations on the Silver Anniversary of the Museum of International Folk Art. During its twenty-five years the museum has proven repeatedly to be a cultural resource without peer for New Mexico, the United States and the world; and on behalf of all New Mexicans, I extend best wishes to the Folk Art Museum for continued growth and development for many years to come.

Sincerely,

JERRY APODACA
Governor

Dear Yvonne:

The Museum of International Folk Art's vigorous performance during its first twenty-five years is a source of pride to the Educational Finance and Cultural Affairs Department.

I extend our warmest congratulations to the museum staff and our sincere hopes for similar high achievement in the years to come.

Sincerely,

HARRY WUGALTER
Secretary for Educational Finance and Cultural Affairs

Dear Yvonne,

In the first twenty-five years of its life, the Museum of International Folk Art has grown in size and stature into an institution in which Florence Dibell Bartlett, its founder, would certainly take pride today.

The museum serves our state in two important ways: it preserves and exhibits the rich folk art traditions of Hispanic New Mexico, and also provides visitors with an opportunity to enjoy folk art from the world community.

On the occasion of the museum's Silver Jubilee, the Board of Regents extends its warmest congratulations and reaffirms its commitment to developing an institution based on the highest standards of excellence.

Sincerely,

TIBO CHAVEZ
President, Board of Regents of the Museum of New Mexico

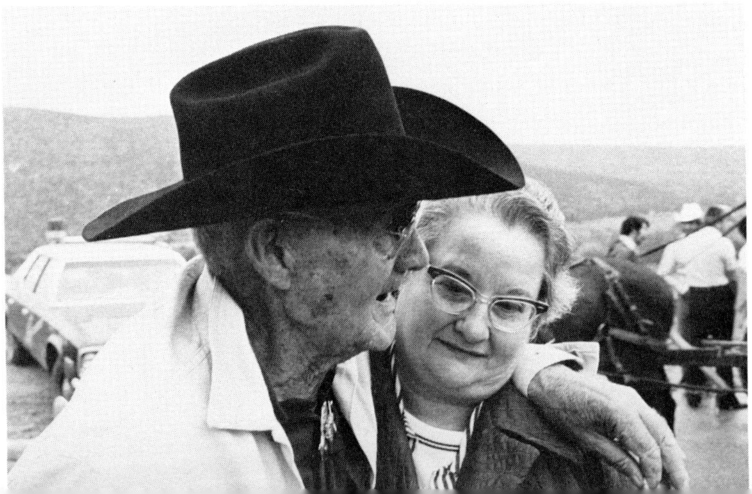

Dr. Yvonne Lange, Director of the Museum of International Folk Art, receives an embrace from Rafael Salinas of the sheriff's posse at the dedication of the Bicentennial tapestry at Villanueva, New Mexico in July, 1976.

People: A Directory

BOARD OF REGENTS,
MUSEUM OF NEW MEXICO:

Tibo J. Chavez, *President;* Mrs. Walter M. Mayer, *Vice President;* Mrs. Edmundo R. Delgado, *Secretary;* Father Benedicto Cuesta, Mrs. Roy A. Downey, Tony Reyna, and Dr. J. Paul Taylor, *Members.*

DIRECTOR OF THE MUSEUM OF NEW MEXICO:

George H. Ewing

STAFF, MUSEUM OF INTERNATIONAL FOLK ART:

Yvonne Lange, Ph.D., *Director;* Paul Winkler, *Assistant Director;* Charlene Cerny, *Curator of American and Latin American Folk Art;* Judith Cohen, *Curator of European Folk Art Collections;* Nora Fisher, *Curator of Textiles;* Christine Mather, *Curator of Spanish Colonial Art;* Carol Steiro, *Curator of Collections;* Alan Vedder, *Conservator;* Ann Bancroft and Judith Sellars, *Librarians;* Lorraine Cook, *Secretary;* Mary Lou Romero, *Secretary/Bookkeeper;* Roger Lovato, *Gallery Attendants Supervisor;* Andrew Abhold, Charles Cizek, Dan Lovato, Robert Quintana, Robert Rael, and Oliver Valdez, *Gallery Attendants.*

BOARD OF TRUSTEES,
INTERNATIONAL FOLK ART FOUNDATION:

Mrs. J. Carrington Woolley, *President;* Mrs. David B. Hall, *Vice President;* Henry R. Hoyt, *Secretary;* Frank M. Bond, *Treasurer;* F. Van Deren Coke, Mrs. Paul C. Frank, Mrs. T. L. Thomas, Mrs. Sallie R. Wagner, *Trustees.*

Administrative Staff: Bonita B. Ellis, Wirt V. Squires, Jr., and Shirley L. Christensen.

FOLK ART COMMITTEE,
MUSEUM OF NEW MEXICO FOUNDATION:

Mrs. Abel Davis, *Chairperson;* Mrs. Harold M. Agnew, Tibo J. Chavez, Fr. Benedicto Cuesta, Mrs. Jeff Good, Mrs. Morton Kligerman, Mrs. James Lilienthal, Mrs. Link Marks, Mrs. Walter M. Mayer, Mrs. Albert G. Simms, Mrs. Kent Tidmore, *Members.*

DIRECTORS,
MUSEUM OF INTERNATIONAL FOLK ART:

Robert Bruce Inverarity, Ph.D.	1949-1954
William J. Lippincott	1954-1957
Edward Ferdon, Jr.	1957-1960
William Friedman	1960-1961
James Taylor Forrest	1961-1963
Delmar M. Kolb, Ph.D.	1963-1966
Charles Proctor	1966-1971
Yvonne Lange, Ph.D.	1971-present

A portion of the spectacular mask collection waits in the storage area in the Museum of International Folk Art.

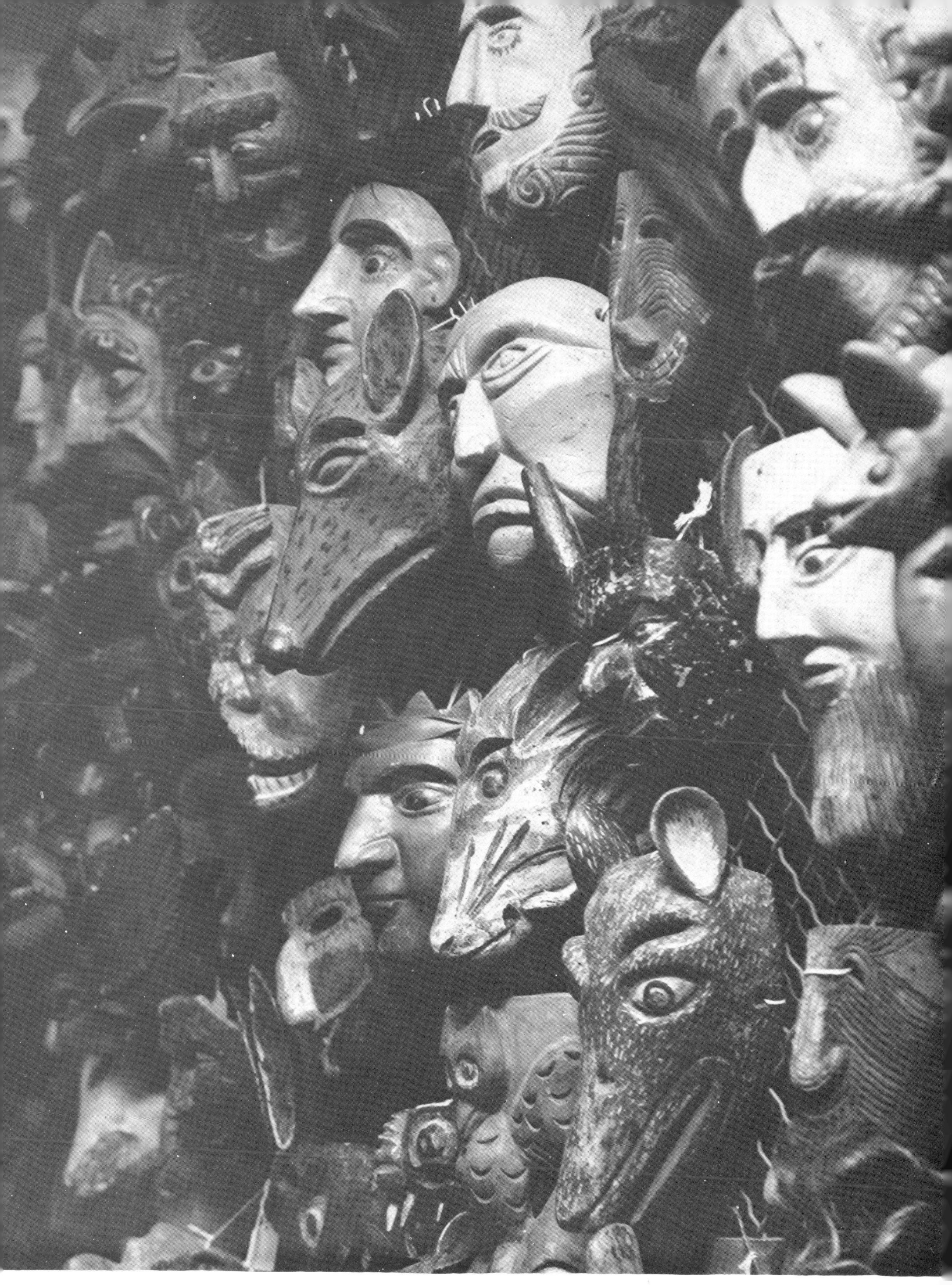